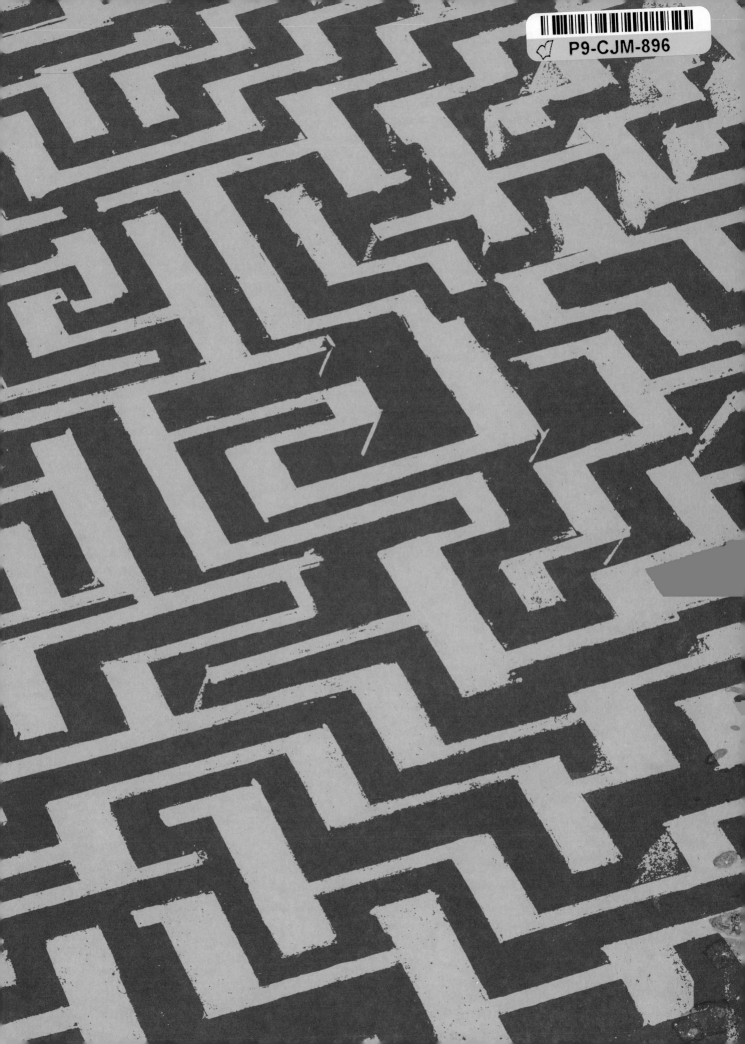

MYSTERIES OF THE ANCIENTS

QUEST FOR THE UNKNOWN

MYSTERIES OF THE ANCIENTS

THE READER'S DIGEST ASSOCIATION, INC.
Pleasantville, New York/Montreal

Quest for the Unknown
Created, edited, and designed by DK Direct Limited

A DORLING KINDERSLEY BOOK

DK DIRECT LIMITED

Series Editor Richard Williams
Senior Editor Sue Leonard; **Editor** Deirdre Headon
Editorial Research Julie Whitaker

Senior Art Editor Susie Breen
Designers Juliette Norsworthy, Alison Verity
Senior Picture Researcher Frances Vargo; **Picture Assistant** Sharon Southren

Editorial Director Jonathan Reed; **Design Director** Ed Day
Production Manager Ian Paton

Volume Consultant Dr. Jennifer Westwood
Commissioning Editor Peter Brookesmith
Contributors Peter Brookesmith, Paul Devereux, Humphrey Evans, Nicholas Jones, Robert Kiener,
John Michell, Steve Moore, Nigel Pennick, Prof. Archie E. Roy, Colin Wilson

Illustrators Jo Agis, Jonathan Bentley, Roy Flooks, Peter Massey,
Steve Rawlings, Sallie Alaine Reason, Mike Shepherd, Tess Stone
Photographers Lindsay Cameron, Simon Farnhell, Mark Hamilton, Alex Wilson

Library of Congress Cataloging in Publication Data

Mysteries of the ancients.
        p.   cm. — (Quest for the unknown)
    Includes index.
    ISBN 0-89577-529-8
    1. Civilization, Ancient.   I. Reader's Digest Association.
    II. Series.
    CB311.M925 1993
    930—dc20   93-8399

Printed in the United States of America

FOREWORD

*A*NCIENT PEOPLES HAVE LEFT THEIR MARK all over the world in monuments and glorious relics. Such creations often provide a tantalizing glimpse of the dazzling achievements of our ancestors. In China we marvel at the underground army of terra-cotta soldiers that guarded the tomb of the First Emperor of China; at Giza we wonder at the construction of the pyramids by the ancient Egyptians; and in what is modern-day Bulgaria we admire the amazingly precocious metalworking skills of the mysterious Thracians.

How did our primitive ancestors produce such miracles? And why? *Mysteries of the Ancients* presents some of the answers. For example, one of the most challenging enigmas is the origin of the different peoples of the world. In this volume, we explore the intriguing links that may exist between cultures separated by vast geographical distances. By looking at the myths and legends of different peoples we may glimpse something of their inner life and preoccupations.

Some suggest that an as yet unknown but sophisticated early civilization, such as the legendary Atlantis, may explain the amazing achievements of the ancients. Others warn against underestimating the ingenuity of human-kind. Modern scientific techniques and scholarship continue to add to our understanding of ancient civilizations. But as each mystery is solved, new ones are unearthed — and many of the answers will always remain lost in the mists of time.

— *The Editors*

CONTENTS

FOREWORD
5

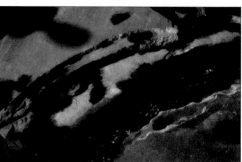

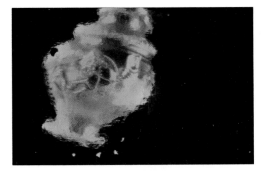

THE SEVEN WONDERS OF THE WORLD

In ancient times seven mighty monuments were known as the wonders of the world. Now that most have disappeared, or lie in ruins, researchers wonder how they were built and what they looked like.

As modern-day air travelers approach Cairo International Airport they are treated to an awe-inspiring view. Bathed in sunshine, and surrounded by two lesser pyramids in a sea of sand, the Great Pyramid at Giza towers majestically over the desert. The 480-foot-tall pyramid, a monument to the pharaoh Khufu, has amazed all those who have seen it since it was built about 2560 B.C. It is also remarkable in another way.

The Great Pyramid is the sole survivor of the Seven Wonders of the Ancient World. The other wonders included: the Hanging Gardens of Babylon; the Statue of Zeus at Olympia; the Temple of Artemis at Ephesus; the Mausoleum at Halicarnassus; the Colossus of Rhodes; and the Lighthouse at Alexandria. This list of marvels was compiled by Philo of Byzantium, an engineer who lived in the late third century B.C. He described each in detail.

Marvelous monuments

We have only the accounts of Philo of Byzantium and other ancient writers to convey the splendor of the monuments. For, apart from the Great Pyramid, ruins are all that remain today of the Seven Wonders of the Ancient World. Excavations of the sites increase our knowledge of what these edifices might have looked like, and leave us marveling at the awesome skill of ancient builders.

The locations of the Seven Wonders of the Ancient World

Halicarnassus   Ephesus
Olympia
Rhodes
Babylon
Alexandria
Giza

THE HANGING GARDENS OF BABYLON

Millions of tumbling plants cascading like a waterfall of greenery from lofty terraces of stone. Man-made mountains planted with a bewildering variety of trees and plants. Trees laden with fruit ripening under the Middle Eastern sun. Ancient writers have thus described the legendary Hanging Gardens of Babylon, the greatest marvel to be found within that great walled city, which was located near the town of Al Hilla, south of Baghdad in modern Iraq.

> ## "Within his palace Nebuchadnezzar erected lofty stone terraces, in which he reproduced mountain scenery by planting them with trees."
>
> **Berossus, third century B.C.**

Legend has it that King Nebuchadnezzar II (604–562 B.C.), a highly innovative and tireless builder, constructed the gardens to remind his homesick Persian wife of the mountains of her native land.

When the site of Babylon was first uncovered at the end of the 19th century by the German archeologist Robert Koldeway, he could find no trace of the flowers or trees that grew in the Hanging Gardens. Nor do any texts that survive from ancient Babylon make any mention of the Hanging Gardens.

Vivid descriptions

Everything we know about the fabled Hanging Gardens of Babylon comes from early writers. Berossus, a priest of the Babylonian deity Marduk who lived in Babylon during the third century B.C.,

tells how Nebuchadnezzar had "knolls made of stone which he shaped like mountains and planted with all kinds of trees...and, within his magnificent palace the king erected lofty stone terraces, in which he reproduced mountain scenery, completing the resemblance by planting them with trees and constructing the so-called Hanging Garden."

Philo of Byzantium described the Hanging Gardens as being made up of tiers of platform terraces, possibly 100 feet square, which were planted with a multitude of trees and plants. The quadrangular gardens were enclosed by 22-foot thick earthen walls. Another writer, the Roman Quintus Curtius Rufus, claimed that: "A distant spectator of these groves would suppose them to be woods nodding on their mountains."

Lost without trace

However, one tangible piece of evidence supporting the existence of the gardens was discovered by Koldeway at Babylon. He found a deep well that resembled no other known ancient well. Koldeway surmised that it had been specially designed for the gardens and that water had been drawn up from it by means of a chain pump. Early writers briefly describe mechanical devices for drawing water for the gardens.

The Hanging Gardens of Babylon may have long since vanished. But there is no doubt that in their full flower they were, in the words of Philo of Byzantium, "a work of art of royal luxury."

PLACE OF SHADE

"On the summit of the citadel are the Hanging Gardens...they equal in height the walls of the town, and their numerous lofty trees afford a grateful shade. The trees are twelve feet in circumference, and fifty feet in height; nor, in their native soil, could they be more productive."
Quintus Curtius Rufus,
History of Alexander
(First century A.D.)

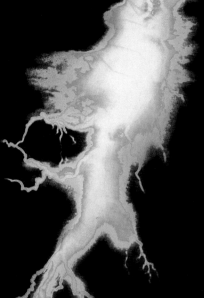

THE STATUE OF ZEUS AT OLYMPIA

Imagine that it is the year 456 B.C. You are entering the ancient Greek temple that stood in the city of Olympia, in southern Greece. Passing between the temple's massive columns, surmounted by brightly painted moldings, you would be confronted by a huge seated figure, which appeared seven times the height of a man. This was the majestic statue of Zeus, the greatest of all the Greek gods.

Zeus's flesh was represented by ivory plates, which were pieced together and supported by a wooden framework, leading Philo of Byzantium to comment that it must have been for this reason that nature had created elephants. Zeus was depicted wearing a robe made of

> ## The sculptor Phidias prayed to Zeus for a sign that the work was acceptable. A bolt of lightning flashed down from the heavens — proof indeed that Zeus approved of his likeness.

gold. On his head rested a sculpted wreath of olive sprays. In his right hand was a statue of a winged figure which represented the goddess Victory, and in his left, a scepter topped by an eagle.

The figure of the god was seated on a throne decorated with gold and precious stones. Friezes of scenes from Greek mythology surrounded the throne.

Legendary sculptor

The legendary Greek sculptor Phidias is said to have toiled for more than five years on the statue. Much of the work was carried out at his workshop near the temple. In 1958 archeologists excavating a garbage dump near the site of this workshop found sculpting tools, and the terra-cotta molds that were used for the statue's drapery, and even a broken jug inscribed: "I belong to Phidias."

And his contemporaries, so the legend goes, judged Phidias's breath-taking statue of the god to be so lifelike that they speculated that Phidias must have seen the deity himself in order to create such a convincing representation.

When Phidias had completed the statue, the story continues, he prayed to Zeus for a sign that the work was acceptable. A bolt of lightning flashed down from the heavens — proof indeed that Zeus approved of his likeness.

Cackle of laughter

The statue of Zeus drew visitors from far and wide after it was placed in the temple at Olympia in 456 B.C. During the first century A.D. the Roman emperor Caligula ordered that the statue be transported to Rome. According to the Roman historian Suetonius, Caligula's biographer, the statue was being made ready to be shipped to Rome when it: "suddenly emitted such a cackle of laughter that the scaffolding collapsed and the workmen fled."

In A.D. 391 the emperor Theodosius I, who had converted to Christianity, out-lawed all pagan cults and ordered all of the temples in the Roman Empire to be closed. The statue was dismantled and transported to Constantinople (modern-day Istanbul). In A.D. 462 it was destroyed by a great fire that raged through the city. Not one fragment of the statue survived. Its likeness, however, was reproduced on countless coins of the time, some of which have been unearthed. And these, together with eyewitness descriptions, are all that remain of the spectacular masterpiece created by Phidias.

THE TEMPLE OF ARTEMIS

In the fifth century B.C., visitors, or pilgrims, approaching the ancient city of Ephesus, which stood near the modern village of Seljuq in southwestern Turkey, would have been unable to miss the magnificent gleaming temple that was dedicated to the Greek goddess Artemis, the patroness of childbirth.

The temple, which was one of the ancient world's most famous places of worship, was renowned for its imposing size. According to the Roman writer Pliny the Elder, "the length of the temple overall is 425 feet, and its breadth 255 feet." The rectangular inner temple was surrounded on all sides by a colonnade, made up of 127 60-foot-high, slender, fluted columns. Marble steps were built around the entire construction.

Flanked by Amazons

The statues of two Amazons flanked the center door. (According to one legend, the Amazons, a race of female warriors, founded the temple.) Inside, a sacrificial altar was set up within the larger altar court, while the house of the goddess stood in the center of the temple.

The jewel-encrusted image of the goddess Artemis, which can be seen on coins found at Ephesus, occupied pride of place in the temple. There are accounts that describe how the statue was taken out from the temple to take part in processions to celebrate the goddess's birthday, or to attend public events such as athletic games and dramatic performances. The temple was built about 565 B.C. by the Greek architect Chersiphron of Knossos, who, according to legend, was assisted in the task by the goddess herself. It soon attracted many pilgrims and visitors.

The temple was also a place of sanctuary to those seeking asylum. The Persian king Xerxes sent his children to the temple for safekeeping after he was defeated in battle by the Greeks in 480 B.C.

In A.D. 262 the Goths sacked Ephesus and destroyed the Temple of Artemis. In A.D. 401 St. John Chrysostom, the archbishop of Constantinople, razed the ruins. The stones were picked over and used as building materials for the rest of the city. Finally nature completed the destruction that humankind had begun. Over the years all that remained

> ## The rectangular inner temple was surrounded on all sides by a colonnade, made up of 127 60-foot-high, slender, fluted columns.

of the once gleaming Temple of Artemis slowly sank into the marshy ground on which the temple had been built.

Temple unearthed

For the next 1,600 years the world thought it had lost forever what the 18th-century English historian Edward Gibbon called "that sacred and magnificent structure." Then, in 1867, the pioneering English archeologist John Turtle Wood, while excavating on the site of the city of Ephesus, unearthed a foundation block of a temple column in deep alluvial mud. Since then, archeologists' finds have enabled them to build up a very accurate model of what the Temple of Artemis might once have looked like.

SECURE FOUNDATIONS

"The temple was built on marshy soil so that it might not be subject to earthquakes or be threatened by subsidences.... To ensure that the foundations of so massive a building would not be laid on shifting, unstable ground, they were underpinned with a layer of closely trodden charcoal, and then with another of sheepskins with their fleeces unshorn."
Pliny the Elder,
Natural History, Book 36
(C. A.D. 77)

THE MAUSOLEUM AT HALICARNASSUS

When Mausolus, the Persian governor of the province of Caria, in present-day southwestern Turkey, died in 352 B.C., his griefstricken widow, Artemisia, set about directing the construction of a great monument that was to be his final resting place, at Halicarnassus (the modern town of Bodrum). This was completed in accordance with her late husband's wishes. The tomb itself was so magnificent that the term *mausoleum* has been used ever since to describe any large and impressive tomb.

Excavations of the site and descriptions in ancient texts give an accurate picture of the grandeur of the mausoleum. The tomb was rectangular, with sides 120 and 100 feet long. Its 60-foot-high walls were topped with a colonnade of 36 Ionic marble columns. (An Ionic column has twin, spiral moldings, like a ram's horns, at the top.) A pyramid-shaped roof completed the imposing structure, while a sculpture of a four-horse chariot crowned the edifice. The entire building reached a staggering height of 140 feet. Much of the tomb was built of blocks of distinctive green volcanic stone.

Dazzling decorations

The most outstanding feature of the mausoleum was its wealth of sculptured decoration. According to the Roman writer Pliny the Elder, writing in the first century A.D., four famous Greek sculptors — Scopas, Bryaxis, Timotheus, and Leochares — contributed works; each was assigned one side of the tomb. There were lions, traditional guardians of tombs; horses; humans (including a statue possibly of Mausolus himself); and friezes of a chariot race and a battle.

The frieze of the chariot race is masterly, showing long-haired charioteers urging on teams of galloping horses. Some of the sculptures have survived, and can be seen in the British Museum in London.

Plundered tomb

By most accounts, the mausoleum survived largely intact until the 13th century A.D., when an earthquake brought down the roof and the colonnade. Later, in 1494, the site was plundered as a rich source of building materials by the Knights of St. John, known as the Knights Hospitalers, who were fortifying their castle at Bodrum. Much of the castle walling, which can still be seen today, is built from the mausoleum's green volcanic stone blocks.

Sadly, many of the tomb's marble sculptures and facing blocks were broken and burnt to make lime for mortar. In 1522 the Knights Hospitalers discovered the intact burial chamber of Mausolus. A French traveler, Claude Guichard, wrote an account of this remarkable find later in the 16th century. It makes tragic reading.

After uncovering the entrance to an underground chamber, the Knights Hospitalers found "bands of marbles of different colors, ornamented with moldings and sculptures which matched the rest of the work...battle scenes were also represented in relief. Having admired this at first, and entertained their fancy with the singularity of the work, they pulled it down, broke it apart and smashed it, in order to use it for the same purpose as the rest."

> The most outstanding feature of the mausoleum was its sculptured decoration. There were lions, horses, humans, and friezes of a chariot race and a battle.

COMPETING SCULPTORS
"That this work is among the seven wonders is due mainly to the artists. The queen died before they finished: but the artists did not abandon the work until it was completed, judging that it would be a monument of their own glory and of their art: and to this day their hands compete."
Pliny the Elder,
Natural History, Book 36
(c. A.D. 77)

THE COLOSSUS OF RHODES

The largest known statue of antiquity stood on the small Greek island of Rhodes in the Aegean Sea. The Colossus of Rhodes was a towering 110 feet tall. The people of Rhodes are said to have erected the statue of their patron deity, Helios, the sun god, in thanks for his help in raising the siege that was laid to the island by the forces of King Demetrius of Macedonia in 305 B.C. The sculptor Chares of Lindos was commissioned to design and erect the bronze statue. According to Philo of Byzantium, the artist's first challenge was simply to locate enough bronze for the work. Chares, Philo wrote, "expended as much bronze on it as seemed likely to create a dearth in the mines: for the casting of the statue was an operation in which the bronze industry of the whole world was concerned."

Massive construction

Chares built a framework of iron and stone. He then, according to Philo, fixed the feet to a white marble base and cast each succeeding part of the statue on top of the previous one. After casting, a mound of earth was heaped around the partially completed statue to provide a base for the next level.

Ancient sources give many details of how the statue was constructed, but little is certain about the form the statue took or what it looked like. Some have suggested that it might have had the head of the god Helios, as depicted on Rhodian coins of the time.

The notion that the colossus had straddled Rhodes's Mandraki Harbor gained some credence in the Middle Ages. However, experts point out that this is impossible since the span of the statue's legs would have had to cover a distance of some 1,300 feet. It seems most likely that the colossus stood in the town itself. Experts believe the figure stood upright with a spear in one hand and a torch in the other.

In 226 B.C. an earthquake shook Rhodes and the colossus toppled to the ground, only 56 years after it had been erected. Ptolemy III of Egypt is alleged to

> It seems most likely that the colossus stood in the town itself. Experts believe the figure stood upright with a spear in one hand and a torch in the other.

have offered to pay for its restoration. But the Rhodians declined his offer. It lay where it fell for nearly nine centuries until, in A.D. 654, Rhodes was invaded by the Arabs, who plundered fragments of the statue. According to tradition, the pieces were shipped to Asia Minor and carried away on the backs of 900 camels. Their whereabouts today is unknown.

THE COLOSSUS
"But even lying on the ground it is a marvel. Few people can make their arms meet round the thumb of the figure, and the fingers are larger than most statues; and where the limbs have broken off enormous cavities yawn, while inside are seen great masses of rock with the weight of which the artist steadied it when he erected it."
Pliny the Elder,
Natural History, Book 34
(c. A.D. 77)

GUIDING LIGHT
"Pharos is an oblong island, is very close to the mainland, and forms with it a harbor with two mouths...the extremity of the isle is a rock, which is washed all round by the sea and has upon it a tower that is admirably constructed of white marble with many stories and bears the same name as the island."
Strabo, The Geography, Book 18
(c. A.D. *24*)

THE LIGHTHOUSE AT ALEXANDRIA

About 2,300 years ago, a vast lighthouse, called the Pharos (meaning lighthouse in Greek), was built on the small flat island, fortified by strong sea walls, to which it gave its name, off the coast of the city of Alexandria, in Egypt. By night its light was said to have been seen for a distance of some 35 miles across the Mediterranean, guiding navigators through the region's dangerous reefs to Alexander the Great's new city. By day its long column of smoke trailed into the sky, marking the location of the port.

The construction of the lighthouse began in 297 B.C. and cost, according to the Roman writer Pliny the Elder, 800 talents of silver (approximately US$3 million in modern currency). Although exact details of how the lighthouse was built are not known, most experts estimate that it was a three-tiered, tapering structure more than 300 feet high, making it the tallest single building of antiquity after the pyramids. The lighthouse was made of white marble, limestone, and reddish-purple granite. On top of it stood a 15-foot statue of Zeus Soter (meaning "Zeus the Savior").

Metal mirrors

Ancient writers claim that the tower's light was provided by a huge fire at its base, which was reflected by mirrors from the top. Some ancient historians believe these were probably highly polished metal sheets, such as burnished bronze, which were frequently used as mirrors in the ancient world.

The question of how the lighthouse keepers supplied the fuel to keep the Pharos's fires burning continues to puzzle historians. Timber was in very short supply in ancient Egypt, which possessed only its native acacia trees and tamarisk shrubs. It is also possible that dried animal dung was used as fuel.

The lighthouse was badly damaged by earthquakes in A.D. 956, 1303, and 1323. By 1349 one Arabian traveler, Ibn Battuta, found the Pharos "in so ruinous a condition that it was not possible to enter it or climb it up to the doorway." Then in 1477 the Sultan Kait Bey built a fort on the site, and many of its remains were used in the construction.

Once-proud building

Even the island of Pharos has long since vanished. Over the centuries it became joined to the mainland by a strip of sand. Today, there is little to remind the visitor to Egypt of the once proud lighthouse other than its representation on ancient coins and mosaics.

That a building of the scale of the Pharos ever existed has tested people's credulity. In the 1920's the English writer E. M. Forster visited the fort that stands where the Pharos once did. He wrote: "Its [the Pharos's] stones have vanished and its spirit also....I tried to multiply its [the fort's] height by five, and thus build up its predecessor. The effort always failed: it did not seem reasonable that so large an edifice should have existed."

Experts estimate the lighthouse was a three-tiered, tapering structure more than 300 feet high, making it the tallest single building of antiquity after the pyramids.

CHAPTER ONE

WHERE DID WE COME FROM?

Humankind has always had an insatiable desire to search for a better life. As a result of this, there is hardly a civilization in the world that does not have, buried in its mythology, the notion that it came from somewhere else.

The ancestors of the native American peoples traveled far to reach their present homelands. Fifteen or twenty thousand years ago, they came, in three great waves, across the land bridge that then existed between Asia and what is now Alaska. From there they slowly made their way throughout the length and breadth of the continent. Some 400 years ago, another

great wave of migration took place, as the first Europeans arrived to take possession of the same lands.

Humans are migratory animals. Even today, 5,000 or more years after the first cities were built, the instinct to move on — to see if the grass is really greener on the other side of the hill — remains firmly part of human psychology.

Settling down
The settled life is still new to humankind. People have only secured their food from farming for 10,000 years at most. About 8000 B.C., some, but not all, communities of Homo sapiens became herders of domestic animals — goats, sheep, and cattle. And farming represented a major change in the way of life of those who took up the new skill.

Before the farming revolution, Homo sapiens had spent perhaps 350,000 years as wanderers. And for possibly 2 million years before that, our earlier human ancestors were constantly moving in order to survive, first as gatherers of food, then as hunters.

Thus for most of its existence, humanity has been on the move. Many human societies are still nomadic gatherers, hunters, and herders. The instinct to migrate is in the very marrow of our bones.

The biblical story of the brothers Cain and Abel (Genesis 4:1–26) symbolizes the disruption caused by the change from the wandering pastoral life to that of the sedentary agriculturalist. Abel's offering of a lamb was more acceptable to the Lord than Cain's offering of "the fruit of the ground." To be "a tiller of the ground," it seemed, was to be slightly

> **In Christianity and in Islam, the long tradition of pilgrimage is allied to the intuition that journeying is essential for the good of the soul.**

unnatural. After Cain slew Abel out of jealousy, he was doomed to be a "fugitive and a vagabond." He settled in the land of Nod — that is, in the wilderness, which had been Abel's natural home.

Opposing habits
The fundamental opposition between the brothers is emphasized by the root meanings of their names. *Abel* means "airy" — something that is constantly in motion. *Cain* derives from the word *kanah*, meaning "to own property." A legend recorded in the Midrash (Hebrew commentaries and interpretative writings relating to the Bible) says that the Lord divided the world between the brothers. Cain owned the land, Abel the creatures. And Abel offended Cain by trespassing on his property, something that Abel could hardly avoid doing.

The very same conflicts still occur today between nomadic peoples and "official" governments, all over the world: the Meo of Southeast Asia, the forest tribes of the Amazon, the Aborigines of Australia, and the Romanies in Europe are all threatened because their outlook is at odds with the "owners" of the land through which they pass.

The first city

In recording the legend of Cain and Abel the ancient Hebrews also implied that town-dwelling was equated with progress and was the acceptable way of life. Cain built the first city, which he called Enoch, for his son.

One of his descendants, Tubal-cain, was a master metalworker; another, the Bible implied, founded the arts of playing the harp and the organ. These are civilized — that is, city-born — pursuits. And then, perhaps most significantly, the Lord marked Cain not as a sign of his sin but rather to protect him against death: "And the Lord put a mark on Cain, lest any who came upon him should kill him" (Genesis 4:15).

Essential journeys

However, the notion of movement, of travel, as both pure and purifying, is buried deep in the human psyche. The Hebrew prophets raged against the waywardness of their urbanized people, urging them to return to their nomadic past and its uncorrupted ways. "Woe to those who join house to house, who add field to field, until there is no more room, and you are made to dwell alone in the midst of the land," says the Lord in the vision of the prophet Isaiah (Isaiah 5:8). Their decadence would continue until "surely many houses shall be desolate, large and beautiful houses, without inhabitant" (Isaiah 5:9).

In Christianity and in Islam, the long tradition of pilgrimage is allied to this intuition that journeying is essential for

Sir William Jones
An engraving from the original painting by the English artist Sir Joshua Reynolds (1723–92). Sir William Jones was the first to point out the similarities among Sanskrit, Latin, and ancient Greek.

the good of the soul. It is a Hindu custom for elderly people to leave their homes and take up the life of a wandering beggar. In folk traditions all over the world, the wise man, the magician, the healer, is described as homeless and peripatetic. An example is the Irish saint, Brendan, and his legendary voyages in the Atlantic Ocean, while in the 20th century the English writer J. R. R. Tolkien drew on the same tradition to create the wizard Gandalf the Grey in *The Lord of the Rings*.

Humankind's seemingly irrepressible desire to move has created more than one mystery for prehistorians. It is certainly not easy to answer the question: Where did we come from?

The problem is partly that there is not enough archeological evidence to chart successfully the movements of the various peoples in prehistory. The best clues we have are linguistic ones. Today roughly half the earth's population speaks a language belonging to a so-called Indo-European group of languages that originated with a long-lost people who lived somewhere in Europe or Asia, possibly as long as 10,000 years ago.

Prehistorians have been baffled by the problem of where, exactly, the ancestor of the family of languages known as "Indo-European" arose, and who spoke it.

Common language

The first person to realize that a single family of languages was spoken from India to Ireland was the 18th-century English orientalist Sir William Jones. In 1786 he remarked in an address to the Asiatic Society of Bengal (where he was serving as a High Court

Arab nomad
Life has changed little since biblical times for the desert nomads of the Middle East, who continue to lead a wandering existence, moving their tents from camp to camp.

judge) on the extraordinary similarities among the ancient Indian language of Sanskrit, Latin, and ancient Greek. This insight lit a fire of scholarly curiosity that has been blazing ever since.

Family ties
Since Sir William's breakthrough, it has become clear that many more languages belong to this Indo-European group: Hittite, English, German, Dutch, Armenian, the Romance languages of France, Romania, Italy, and Iberia, the Celtic tongues, the Scandinavian

Linguistic clues
This relief shows a Hittite queen and her child, and some Hittite text. Hittite was thought to be an Indo-European language because its endings for nouns and verbs are similar to those of other early Indo-European languages.

languages, the Slavic languages, and Albanian. In the east, the Farsi language spoken in Iran and Afghanistan, and the Hindi, Urdu, Sindi, Nepali, and Bengali (among others) of India itself, all belong to the same Indo-European family.

Many questions still vex linguists and archeologists: Where did the proto-Indo-European language originate? Did its speakers ever exist as a single people? An additional problem for linguists was how did their language, or its descendants, make its way across two continents? Was it borne on horseback by columns of conquerors, or did it seep slowly, through trade and diplomacy, from its mysterious birthplace?

Although 20th-century academics have proposed various theories as to the

origins of the ancestral Indo-European language, there is no clear explanation. Most scholars have attempted to combine clues from existing archeological and linguistic knowledge to reach some workable hypothesis.

Sanskrit, Hittite, Latin, Persian, and ancient Greek were all fully developed before 1000 B.C. The rich variety and antiquity of these languages suggest that their common ancestor was far older, and most researchers agree that they had become separate tongues between 3000 and 2000 B.C. So the search has been for a population that probably started from small beginnings but expanded throughout the area between southern Europe and central Asia from about 3000 B.C.

> Was the ancestral Indo-European language borne on horseback by columns of conquerors or did it seep slowly, through trade and diplomacy, from its mysterious birthplace?

Other limiting factors are that the mystery language seemed to have no word for the sea, although it did have words for wolves, snow, trees, bears, horses, and chariots. An inland, forest-dwelling, equestrian — and probably warrior — culture seems to be the best candidate. In 1902 the German archeologist Gustav Kossinna claimed to have archeological evidence supporting his theory that the language was born in Germany.

Perfect solution
Other scholars favored the notion of a race of blond, blue-eyed Aryans, whose physical and intellectual superiority enabled them to spread out from somewhere in northern Europe, conquering as they went. This misguided theory was borrowed and embroidered by the Nazi political movement in Germany, to disastrous effect, in the two decades before the end of the Second World War.

The favorite contenders for the origin of the ancestral Indo-European language

▶ PAGE 28

THE PEOPLE OF ATLANTIS

Why is it that the Basques of northern Spain speak a language that bears no relation to that spoken by other Spaniards? Some Basques claim it is because their language originated in the lost city of Atlantis.

Pelota players
A French magazine illustration from 1902 shows Basque pelota players in action.

FEW PEOPLES OF WESTERN EUROPE escaped the influence of the incoming Indo-European language. Today we know of only two — the long-since-vanished Etruscans of Italy, whose language survives only in imperfectly understood inscriptions, and the fiercely independent Basques, who live in the northern border region between France and Spain.

Logic would say that the Basques are the aboriginal people of the region. Their language, as far as any linguist has been able to judge, bears no relation to any other in the world. Only some 500,000 people speak it. It would be reasonable to suppose that it is a relic of the time before the Iberians, the bearers of Indo-European language and culture, arrived in Spain and France. But, astonishingly, some Basques deny this.

These Basques say that they were not originally a European people at all. In fact, many maintain that they are descended from the survivors of the collapse of Atlantis, the legendary island continent that the Greek philosopher Plato placed in the Atlantic Ocean. *Atlaintika* is the Basque name for the lost continent.

The *Atlantida*, the Basque national epic poem, is the official literary source for this belief. Skeptics point to the fact that the poem was composed in the 19th century, but like many other epics committed to paper long after their first telling, it is based on age-old folk belief and oral tradition.

Ancient language

In *The Secret of Atlantis* (1978), for example, the Viennese scientist Otto Muck cites the German writer Ernst von Salomon's account of a conversation he had in 1930 with an old Basque smuggler. The old man called the Basque tongue "the oldest language in the world" and went on to say that "the Basques are the last relics of a more beautiful, freer, prouder world, long ago sunk beneath the sea."

Is there any independent evidence that the Basques are indeed survivors from the lost continent of Atlantis, or even that Atlantis existed? Those who believe that Atlantis was indeed a lost Atlantic continent argue that there is evidence.

They point out that the method of tilling the soil that the Basques use in Europe is identical to the method used by the ancient Mayans and by some Central American Indians today — dibble cultivation (making holes in the soil for seeds using a small hand implement) rather than plowing. They also point to the striking similarity between the ball game played by the ancient Mayans and pelota, which is still played by Basques today. They further claim that linguistic similarities exist between Basque and several American Indian languages.

The highly speculative conclusion that Muck draws is that "these...similarities form a bond between peoples on two sides of the Atlantic [and they] point to a common cause, a common center: Atlantis, heartland of this long-vanished maritime power."

Vague connections

Skeptics would be less likely to draw the same conclusion. Dibble cultivation is rightly called the crudest known method of agriculture, and it is practiced all over the world where the principles of plowing have not been discovered. The rules of pelota and the sacred Mayan ball game — so far as the latter can be deciphered — are not that dissimilar from many other ancient games (real tennis and the Eton wall game, for example), and the Mayan game was distinctive in that it was played for life or death. As for linguistic similarities, professional linguists would deny that there are any.

Mayan ball player
The ancient Mayans played a ball game similar to the modern Basque game of pelota. But for the Basque players it is not a matter of life or death, as it literally was for their Mayan counterparts.

in most scholars' eyes have been Asia, central Europe, northern Europe, the southern Russian steppes, and Anatolia (eastern Turkey). The evidence for each has been based on the results of intensive linguistic research, supported by archeological evidence. Such evidence ranges from styles of burial and the shapes of battle-axes to the spread of horsemanship.

Since the 1970's the most influential theories have come from Lithuanian-American archeologist Marija Gimbutas, of UCLA, who has argued, largely from evidence found in burial mounds, that the Kurgan people, a semi-nomadic group from north of the Black Sea, first migrated west into Europe and east into Iran about 3000 B.C.

But not everyone agrees. Prof. Colin Renfrew of Cambridge University, England, has argued that the original Indo-Europeans were Anatolians.

Prof. Renfrew argues that the

Civilized language
Unicorn seals from the Indus Valley civilization (c. 3000–1500 B.C.) of Pakistan. Researchers believe that Indus Valley people may have been using the ancestral Indo-European language up to 5,000 years ago.

Anatolian fertility figure
The mother goddess was extremely important to the ancient Anatolians, who looked to her for help with their crops. The Anatolians were such successful farmers that they were able to support a growing population. Eventually the relocation of some Anatolians may have caused the spread of their language.

language did not spread by military force or other organized migration. His theory centers around the Anatolians, ancestors of the Hittites, who were among the first of the Middle Eastern peoples to learn how to farm. As the new means of subsistence was so efficient, it led inevitably to an increase in the population, which then had to expand its living space. Prof. Renfrew calculates that the movement westward may have taken place at a pace of no more than a few miles each year. Land cultivation, beginning in Greece in 6500 B.C., shows a definite, if irregular, movement by various routes westward toward the British Isles and Scandinavia, until 3000 B.C. at the latest, when it reached the Orkneys. The dates when farmers first began tilling the land coincide with changes in other cultural areas from burial practice to mythology.

Impressive invaders
The route, and the causes, of the eastward drive into India are less clear. Prof. Renfrew suggests the language reached India partly by the slow movement of a successful pastoral people in search of new pastures and partly through a later incursion of a more aggressive, horse-riding culture. Whether these latter people were intent on conquest, or — like the Europeans who descended upon the Americas in the 16th century — merely highly inquisitive and acquisitive, they seem to have so greatly impressed the native peoples with their power that the natives adopted the newcomers' language. This last invasion of what is now Pakistan took place about 1500 B.C. However, says Prof. Renfrew, "It is perfectly possible

that the languages used in the Indus Valley civilization as early as 3000 B.C. were already Indo-European."

The issue of the true origins, dates, and reasons for the spread of the Indo-European language is far from settled. Prof. Renfrew admits that much of his argument is speculation. And to accept Prof. Renfrew's theory means accepting a huge shift back in time of events whose dates other scholars have long agreed on. Far from beginning its movement outward about 3000 B.C., Prof. Renfrew suggests, the ancestral Indo-European language would have begun to break up at least 5,000 years before that, if it were to move (westward at any rate) with the new farming culture. However, there is a highly persuasive reason to accept Prof. Renfrew's hypothesis.

"The crux of the issue," writes J. P. Mallory in *In Search of the Indo-Europeans* (1989), "is bilingualism and how it was induced. Without state coercion, we do not imagine that second languages are forced upon people. Rather, bilingualism

> ## "It is perfectly possible that the languages used in the Indus Valley civilization as early as 3000 B.C. were already Indo-European."
> ### Prof. Colin Renfrew

is induced when the context of speech requires the use of the new language if one wishes to obtain better access to goods, status, ritual or security."

The language of commerce
This reason, for example, is why English is the premier international language today. Relatively tiny numbers of English-speaking people administered the old British Empire and captained its powerful merchant marine, and still fewer American businessmen followed in their wake — but these were the people who represented power, wealth, and opportunity. English is now the language of diplomacy and commerce. It is also, like its ancestor, Indo-European, beginning to split up into separate sub-

Astronaut in space
Humankind's tireless desire to travel in search of new resources and new lands continues with the modern-day exploration of space.

languages in different parts of the world. Even American English and British English often use completely different words to describe exactly the same items.

Misleading clue?
Mallory further points out that if the extraordinary advantage of farming skills were being offered by Indo-European speakers, native peoples would have learned the language in order to acquire this new, highly efficient means of securing their survival. This means that the language may have been primarily learned, rather than being passed on through the generations by intermarriage between the newcomers and the natives. It may not, therefore, be such a good clue as to our genetic make-up or racial origins.

It is possible that we shall never discover the heart of this particular mystery. But what the "Indo-European problem" undoubtedly proves is that human beings have never, and probably will never, cure their innate curiosity about what lies over the horizon.

If man is not still fundamentally a wanderer, why then, in the face of numerous problems on earth, did the human race spend billions to take the first steps into space?

Indus sculpture
In 1922, the mounds of Mohenjo Daro on the right bank of the Indus River in Pakistan were excavated. On discovering the remains of a large city, including many artifacts, archeologists realized that they had probably discovered the site of the capital of the Indus Valley civilization.

PACIFIC OCEAN

Asia

North
America

Japan

MALAY ARCHIPELAGO

Philippines

MICRONESIA

Hawaiian Islands

Caroline Islands

MELANESIA

New Guinea

Torres Strait

Marquesas

Tuamotu

Fiji

Samoa

Society Islands

Tonga

POLYNESIA

Australia

New Zealand

| 0 | 200 | 400 | | 800 | | 1200 | | 1600 | | 2000 | | 2400 | | 2800 | Miles |

| 0 | 400 | 800 | | 1600 | | 2400 | | 3200 | | 4000 | | Kilometers |

LOST IN THE MISTS OF TIME

There are peoples whose mysterious origins have led to much speculation about where they originally came from.

THE TRUE ORIGINS of the scattered population of the Polynesian islands in the south Pacific are unknown. It is unclear where they came from, and far from obvious how such a homogenous people spread so far and wide. The Polynesians are similar in looks, culture, and language, yet thousands of miles of ocean separate them.

There is no lack of theories to explain their origins. One of the earliest proposed that they came from Asia by way of the south Pacific and colonized Central and South America before moving on to the islands of Polynesia. But there is little similarity between the language, customs, or appearance of the Polynesians and the South American Indians.

In the late 1940's the Norwegian explorer Thor Heyerdahl proved that it had been possible for seafarers in ancient times to travel west from South America to Polynesia. His raft *Kon-Tiki* sailed from Peru to Tuamotu. But this feat proved only that the voyage was indeed possible, not that it had been made a significant number of times.

Possible theories

Most modern experts agree that the Polynesians came from somewhere in Asia. One theory suggests that their culture first developed in Malaysia as a mixture of Southeast Asian agriculture with rituals and beliefs derived from India and China. Racially, this people was a combination of Mongoloids and Caucasoids. Pushed eastward by war, population pressure, or sheer curiosity, they may have taken to the sea. Avoiding New Guinea, they could have made their way through Micronesia and within a few generations made landfall on Samoa and the Society Islands. From these two centers, they could have spread throughout the rest of Polynesia, north to Hawaii and south to New Zealand.

Waves of colonization

Another theory proposes that the physical traits of the Polynesians are the result of a mixture of two waves of colonization. The first wave, of dark-skinned people, could have come through Melanesia, maybe from India; the second wave, of lighter-skinned people, came perhaps from Southeast Asia, bringing Chinese influences.

Simultaneous colonization may have been the result of a large fleet setting out eastward in the sheer hope of finding new lands.

But it seems likely that the islands were settled at more or less the same time. Pottery of the same age has been found in the island groups of both Tonga and the Marquesas — at the western and eastern extremities of the island groups.

This simultaneous colonization may have been the result of a large fleet setting out eastward in the sheer hope

of finding new lands, and twice striking lucky. Or such a fleet could have split up, perhaps in a storm, one part reaching Tonga while the other continued until, at last, it came to the Marquesas.

Sailing tradition
A sailing canoe off the Caroline Islands in the south Pacific.

South America

31

Although traditional Polynesian sailing craft — which can be big enough to carry 100 adults and provisions — are highly seaworthy, they are also immensely difficult to handle and hold on course against a head wind. And the sailors' ability to chart their position in open water would have been no more than guesswork. So it is possible that many of the islands were settled by accident, by sailors being blown off course on what were intended to be short voyages.

It is even possible that the whole of the Polynesian colonization started with one boatload of Southeast Asian travelers, well-stocked with goods to trade, being blown far into the Pacific and eventually making a lucky landfall. However the Polynesian people began, it is clear that their impressive sailing ships carried both men and women.

Abundance of hair

Farther north in the Pacific live another mystery people — the Ainu of Japan. Now confined to the northernmost islands, the Ainu were once to be found all over the northern half of the Japanese archipelago. They are physically unlike the Japanese, speak a unique language, and have an entirely different religion, centered on their chief god, the bear. They are also remarkable for the abundance of their body hair.

It remains unclear whether their ancestors or those of the Japanese were the first to colonize the islands. The Japanese islands were, in all likelihood, on the very same route of the Mongoloid peoples who crossed the ancient land bridge between Asia and North America to colonize the New World. Some pre-historians have even speculated that the Ainu were one of the migrating peoples who stayed on the west coast of the Pacific. Other historians, however, have suggested that they were established there before those migrations began.

Various theories have proposed links between the Ainu and Indo-European, western Asian, and Mongoloid peoples —

and even the Australian Aborigines. It is also possible that they are entirely unique, a remnant of a genetic strain that, wherever it came from, remained isolated from the rest of humanity. Now, however, Ainu (the word, poignantly, means simply "person") is no longer spoken as a first language, and the Ainu people have been actively encouraged to mix with the Japanese population.

No less mysterious than other Pacific peoples are those of Australia. One of the key questions to be asked is when did the Aborigines first arrive in Australia. If, on the one hand, they arrived during the last great Ice Age, which lasted from

Ainu man
It has been suggested that the Ainu people of Japan and Australian Aborigines shared common ancestors. There is no disputing the fact that some representatives of the two peoples look alike.

Desert hunter
An Australian Aborigine holds the all-purpose hunting and warring implement — the boomerang.

about 20,000 to 10,000 years ago, the journey between New Guinea (the nearest landmass) and the continent could have been made largely on foot, as there was a land bridge between the continents, which is now sunk beneath the Torres Strait. Sea levels were lower, with the result that there were only short stretches of water between the islands of Malaysia, Indonesia, and the Philippines.

If, on the other hand, the Aborigines arrived after the Ice Age, the only route possible would have been by sea. Thus, it is an open question whether they came through the Malay Archipelago and Java or down the Asian Pacific coast. Most researchers now believe that the eastern route via New Guinea is more and more unlikely — because the prevailing winds would have blown them out into the Pacific, not south or west to Australia. Furthermore, Aboriginal culture seems to have fanned out across Australia from the northwest, not the northeast.

The second key question is: Why did the Aborigines migrate south? Whenever they did so, there is no evidence that population pressure pushed them in that direction. So would they have ventured into the unknown ocean — Australia and Timor, the easternmost Indonesian Island, are 400 miles apart — in frail craft out of sheer curiosity? Many prehistorians believe that they would not have done so, and they employ this argument as evidence that the Aborigines arrived in Australia by accident. Yet perhaps the answer lies in humankind's naturally curious, and often reckless, nature.

The Indonesian monsoon — which blows from the northwest — might have blown a canoe off course, to make land-fall on the Kimberley or Arnhem coasts. This could have happened at any time during or after the last Ice Age, up to 4,000 years ago. The cultural and physical homogeneity of the Aborigines suggests that few people were involved. They also had at least two dogs with them, since dogs — now wild dingoes — seem to have arrived in Australia with man.

Common ancestors
But where did they originally come from? One theory suggests that the Aborigines and the Ainu are descendants of common ancestors and that the Aborigine's immediate ancestors came south from the Yellow Sea through the Philippines, mainly on foot, partly by sea. However, there is no evidence that anyone

> Many prehistorians believe there is evidence that the Aborigines arrived in Australia by accident.

remotely like the Aborigines settled in New Guinea before the current Melanesian inhabitants — who are physically quite different.

Similar-looking peoples
There is, however, a similar-looking people to the Aborigines who dwell in Ceylon and southern India. They are the Dravidian hill tribes — and they also use boomerangs. Prof. A. A. Abbie of Adelaide University, Australia, has argued that both the Dravidians and the Aborigines are descended from a "proto-Caucasoid" people from central Asia, who, about 20,000 years ago, first began to migrate: west, to become the "Indo-Europeans;" south to become the Dravidians; east to become the Ainu; and southeast, through Burma, Thailand, and the Malay Archipelago, to become the very first Australians. Hill tribes along this route, called Negritoes, look strikingly similar to southern Indian tribes and the Aborigines. Prof. Abbie claims that they, too, are relics of that migration.

If Prof. Abbie's supposition is correct, then the first contact between Europeans and Aborigines in the 18th century was, anthropologically and historically, much like the meeting of long-lost cousins.

Yet even if it is possible in theory to trace the beginnings of the Aborigines, the English, and the Ainu to a common source, the basic question remains: Where did they come from before that?

Remote landscape
A Finn employs a traditional method of transport.

LOST AND FOUND
Europe, too, has its mystery peoples. The Basques, who live on the northern borders of France and Spain, have long intrigued anthropologists. While the Basques themselves claim to be remnants of the lost people of Atlantis, orthodox pre-historians suspect that they — like the vanished Etruscans of Italy — are a remnant of Europe's aboriginal peoples.

Uncommon language
Like the Basques, the Finns do not speak an Indo-European language, although they are surrounded by neighbors who do. But the Finns are not aboriginals, and their language is not unique. Finnish belongs to the Finno-Ugric family of languages, which also includes Lapp, Estonian, and Hungarian.

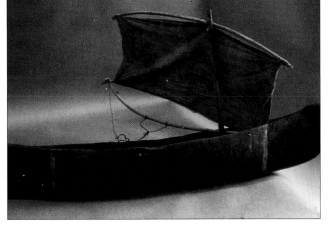

Fragile craft
It has been suggested that many thousands of years ago, the Aborigines arrived in Australia, having traveled hundreds of miles in primitive canoes like this one.

LAND OF THE GIANTS

Giants are considered the stuff of legends, but real giants do exist. And some truly enormous bones, claimed to be human, have also been found.

Artist's impression
This illustration is taken from a 17th-century treatise on giants. The main figure was based on bones found in a Sicilian cave in the 14th century.

THE MOST FAMOUS BIBLICAL GIANT is Goliath the Philistine, who was reported to have been about 10 feet tall (1 Samuel 17:4). Whole tribes, such as the Emim and the Anakim mentioned in Deuteronomy, were also described as giants. Og, king of Bashan, was the last of the legendary giant tribe of Rephaim. His iron bed, the Bible says, measured 6 by 13½ feet and was kept as a "museum piece" at Rabbah, on the Ammonite border (Deuteronomy 3:11).

The ancient skull had a larger brain capacity "than any American within historic times."

The Bible is not the only source of written references to giants. Sacred texts and myths and legends all over the world tell of giant races and individuals, and archeological records seem to support these tales. The records of American state archeological societies in particular contain numerous reports of giant human bones that have been excavated and then ignored or lost. Present-day archeologists, however, are skeptical of most of the evidence for the existence of giants, but despite this, it continues to be brought forward.

During the 1930's, Dr. Ales Hrdlicka of the Smithsonian Institution examined an ancient skull found in the Aleutian Islands off Alaska and reported that its owner had a larger brain capacity "than any American within historic times."

In earlier centuries, numerous gigantic bones were found that early experts were quick to identify as human. Such bones were often exhibited in churches and museums as relics of a giant race that existed before the Flood.

Man or mammoth?
Modern scientists and researchers think that most of these large bones were the remains of large creatures such as mammoths, elephants, and whales. Yet those who first identified them often stressed that they were aware of the difference between giant human and animal bones.

Vanquished giant
The Israelite David is seen holding the head of the Philistine giant Goliath whom he slayed in single combat. This powerful painting is by the 17th-century English painter and poet Thomas Flaxman.

In 1613 a 30-foot tomb was found near St. Antoine in France. The bones within it were identified by an inscription as those of King Teutobochus of Gaul, who had fought against the Romans. Defeated in battle, he had been taken to Rome to participate in a triumphal parade. Witnesses reported that he was so tall, he towered over the trophies that the soldiers carried on their upright lances.

A coffin containing the bones of a giant 19 feet tall was reportedly found under a fallen oak in Lucerne, a province of Switzerland, in 1577. Skeptical scholars, however, claimed that the bones were those of a mastodon or elephant.

There are many stories that, up to the 19th century at least, remnants of the

Patagonian people
Adm. John Byron converses with a giant native woman in this 18th-century engraving. Byron was the grandfather of the English poet Lord Byron, who based his poem Don Juan *on the admiral's exploits in South America.*

old races of giants lingered on in remote corners in the world. In Patagonia, for example, the southernmost tip of South America, travelers in the 16th and 17th centuries reportedly told stories of tribes of giants up to 12 feet tall.

In 1764 the English naval officer Adm. John Byron sailed to Patagonia to investigate these alleged reports, and is said to have encountered a "gigantic" tribe of natives. One of his officers, who was 6 feet 2 inches tall, was allegedly made to feel a "pygmy among giants." Midshipman Clerke, another crew member, estimated the height of the natives to be "certainly nine feet, if they did not exceed it."

Above average
Robert Wadlow standing next to a man of average height.

WHY DO GIANTS EXIST?
Medically, there are two types of giants. The freaks of nature who in less sensitive times appeared in sideshows and circuses generally had an overactive pituitary gland that caused their abnormal size. These are called pituitary giants. Some of the best-known historical examples, all from the late 19th and early 20th centuries, are the American Jack Earle, who was 7 feet 7 inches tall, and Chang, the Chinese giant, who reached a height of 7 feet 8½ inches.

Early death
Perhaps the best-known pituitary giant of all is Robert Pershing Wadlow, who was born in Alton, Illinois, in 1918. Listed in the *Guinness Book of Records* as the Tallest Man in the World, he reached a height of 8 feet 11 inches. Wadlow died when he was only 22, for pituitary giants often suffer from ill-health and rarely survive into old age.

Tall and strong
The other cause of giantism is a particular abnormal grouping of chromosomes, and people who reach excessive heights as a result are called genetic giants. Unlike pituitary giants, genetic giants are perfectly healthy. Into this group fall very tall peoples such as the Watusi tribe of Rwanda, many of whom grow to heights of more than seven feet.

FATHERS OF THEIR PEOPLE

The colorful heroes and villains of ancient myth and legend may tell us more about our past than we realize.

ALL PEOPLES HAVE THEIR OWN mythological versions of where they come from and how their nation was founded. These myths may recount, in magical, divine, or heroic terms, real events that helped form a society — migrations, the invention or discovery of crucial skills, the defeat of adversity; or they may make a special moral point that reflects vital values and attitudes within the society. The deeds of the heroes of myths, legends, and folklore are keys that unlock the code of how a society views itself, what it fears, and what it would most like to be.

The oldest written epic yet discovered is the story of Gilgamesh, who was, in reality, probably the fifth king of the Sumerian city of Uruk. In myth he was a giant 11 cubits tall (a cubit is about 18 inches), with a mighty

> **On the farther shore Gilgamesh is denied immortality but is given a plant that confers ever-recurrent youth. But the plant is stolen from him, as he lies sleeping, by a snake.**

chest nine spans across (a span is the distance from the thumb to the little finger of a spread hand). Gilgamesh was said to be two-thirds god and one-third man. The central preoccupation of the epic of Gilgamesh is death and the great struggle to find a way to defeat it.

Rejoicing in life

Gilgamesh undergoes enormous trials and even crosses the sea that divides life and death in the hope of finding eternal life. On the farther shore he is denied immortality but is given a plant that confers the next best thing, ever-recurrent youth. But the plant is stolen from him, as he lies sleeping, by a snake. The snake puts the plant to good use, which explains why snakes seem to be reborn each year by sloughing off their old skin. Once resigned to his own mortality, however, Gilgamesh learns to rejoice in life.

This is the central moral theme of the epic. But there is another theme that haunts its opening episodes, which concerns a wild man, Enkidu. To understand the

significance of this side of the story, one has to remember that Uruk was one of the world's first cities. It was settled by people who had once been nomads and was surrounded by Bedouin tribes who were herders rather than city-dwelling farmers, merchants, and bureaucrats.

Gilgamesh, ruler of Uruk, is a despot. He enslaves his people to build the walls of his city, crushes them with taxes and unjust laws, and takes whomever he desires — wives, daughters, young men — to relieve his insatiable lust. In the end the long-suffering people call on the gods for assistance, and they create Enkidu as a rival for Gilgamesh. He is as powerfully built as the king but has been left to grow up in the wild. Enkidu has complete sympathy with nature and is uncivilized, his body covered with matted hair.

The 11th tablet
The epic of Gilgamesh was transcribed onto 12 tablets in the seventh century B.C.

Dangerous liaison

When Gilgamesh hears of Enkidu's size and strength, he is instantly jealous and sends a temple prostitute to seduce him. After a week's ceaseless dalliance with the tempting lady, Enkidu finds that the wild animals flee from him. He is no longer at one with nature. Prompted by the prostitute, he then goes to the city of Uruk — partly in the hope of enjoying its fleshpots, partly to challenge Gilgamesh.

Enkidu finds his excuse to fight Gilgamesh when he discovers the king is about to exercise his customary *droit du seigneur* (the right of a ruler to possess a subject's bride on her wedding night). An awesome combat follows, which ends when Gilgamesh fells Enkidu and finds his rage has vanished. The two embrace and become friends. Under Enkidu's influence, Gilgamesh institutes a just rule in Uruk.

Living in harmony

Here, in symbolic form, are laid out the tensions between city and country that are not entirely eradicated today. There is the countryman's vision of the city as the center — and probable cause — of all debauchery and depravity. There is also the fragility of the bond between man and nature and the city dweller's distrust of the free ways of the country. But the Gilgamesh epic also makes plain that each side can learn from the other and live in harmony. And in the episodes that follow, the epic seems to mourn the loss of natural wisdom — symbolized by the eventual death

Out of time
This painting by the 18th-century Japanese artist Kitagawa Kikumare shows Urashima and Princess Otohime. Urashima carries the casket that he later opened to cause his rapid aging.

of Enkidu — that living in the city entails. Our roots are in the country, this vast work reminds us, and we lose touch with the past and what it is able to teach us at our peril.

The Japanese, half a world away from the Sumerians, were also fascinated by the quest for eternal life. Their legend speaks of a young fisherman, Urashima Taro of Mizunoe, who in A.D. 478 saved the life of a tortoise — some versions say a turtle — which in Japanese lore is an emblem of old age and therefore automatically deserving of respect. However, this was no ordinary tortoise. Urashima met the creature again while out in his fishing boat, and they fell into conversation. The tortoise explained that she was Princess Otohime, the daughter of the Dragon King of the Sea, and turned herself into a young woman. Then she took Urashima beneath the waves to visit her father's kingdom.

Fatal farewell
Urashima was so taken with the underwater world, and with Otohime, that he stayed and became her husband. After three years living beneath the sea, he explained to Otohime that he wanted to return home to visit his parents. They were getting on in years, and he wanted to let them know about his marriage. Somewhat reluctantly, Otohime agreed, on condition that he return to her. She then gave him a comb box to take with him, explaining that if he ever opened it he would never see her again.

Urashima made his way back to dry land and to his home village. But it no longer looked the way he remembered it, and he recognized none of the people there. His parents' house had vanished, and no one had ever heard of them. Eventually, he discovered the date, A.D. 825. What had only been three

years to him in the kingdom of the sea had been 347 years on dry land.

In spite of his wife's grave warning, Urashima opened the box she had given him. A thin white plume of smoke curled up from it, and as it did so he aged. Earthly time caught up with Urashima: His skin wrinkled and his hair turned

> # Earthly time caught up with Urashima: His skin wrinkled and his hair turned white, and then his heart stopped.

white, and his heart stopped. Eternal life, for Urashima as for Gilgamesh, had proved to be no more than an illusion.

When asked how their city came to be founded, the ancient Greek citizens of Thebes (now Luxor in Egypt) would give the credit to Cadmus. Indeed the city was first called Cadmea after its founder, who was given a goddess, Harmonia, as his queen. Their nuptials were attended by the Greek gods — the first of only two occasions when they honored a mortal in this way. However, Cadmus brought more to Thebes — and Greece — than a wedding party of feasting gods. He brought the art of writing.

Influential mortal
Cadmus, the founder of the ancient city of Thebes, is shown on this Greek vase.

The name *Cadmus* means "eastern," and Cadmus' father, Agenor, was king of Tyre, in Phoenicia, or Canaan. In Greek myth, Agenor's daughter, Europa, was abducted by Zeus in the shape of a white bull and later ravished by him. Agenor dispatched his sons, Cadmus among them, to recover their sister. Failing in that task, Cadmus was told by the oracle at Delphi to follow a cow with a mark in the shape of a moon on each flank, and to build a city wherever she stopped. He did as he was advised and founded Thebes.

Art of writing

The key to Cadmus' real achievement, introducing the art of writing to the Greeks, lies in his origins as a Phoenician. In *Greek Myths* (1955), the English poet and novelist Robert Graves suggests that the rape of Europa represents Greek invasions of the eastern Mediterranean, while the quest of Cadmus and his brothers for Europa symbolizes the flight of Canaanite tribes away from the invaders.

As a consequence, the Greeks came into contact with Phoenician writing. The Phoenician alphabet consisted solely of consonants, and it was a Greek stroke of genius to adapt some of those letters into signs for vowels, so that the new Greek alphabet represented all the vocal sounds in the Greek language. The mythmakers gave Cadmus of Thebes the credit for this achievement.

Diplomatic marriage

A key Vietnamese legend likewise records the meeting of different peoples in striking, symbolic imagery. The Vietnamese consider their first authentic king to have been Lac Long Quang — Dragon Lord of the Vietnamese. He was the grandson of King De Minh and an immortal mountain fairy. Then, as now, the Vietnamese were in conflict with the Chinese. Lac Long Quang brought peace through a diplomatic marriage with Au Co, a Chinese immortal. Legend says that she bore him 100 eggs, from which hatched 100 sons.

In due course, the couple separated, and they divided their 100 sons equally between them. Lac Long Quang remained in the lowlands, and his son Hung Vuong founded the first royal dynasty in Vietnam, while Au Co and her sons went into the mountains. In the legends of Vietnam they are clearly associated with the immortals; the Dragon Lords are the coastal people. This is a common folklore image among many peoples in Southeast Asia.

Historical event

But the parting of Au Co and Lac Long Quang may represent a specific prehistoric event — a retreat, perhaps because of internal strife, by a group of the original Vietnamese dwellers into the mountains around the Red River Delta. Anthropologists have noted that the language and customs of the Muong people, who live in those mountains now, are closely related to those of the Vietnamese — unlike those of the Meo and other related hill tribes of Vietnam. The Muong people may well be the descendants of the mythical Au Co and her 50 sons.

These tales give but a glimpse of the richness and variety of the ways in which different peoples have explained themselves, their origins, and their achievements. Myth and legend are not reality and are a world apart from academic history, yet they may reveal more than any dry chronicle of events about the real inner life of a people.

Mountain dwellers
A Muong village in Vietnam. It has been suggested that the Muong are descended from Au Co and her 50 sons, who lived in the mountains following their split from their father, Lac Long Quang.

Wild West hero?
An engraving from a photograph of Wyatt Earp taken in the 1880's.

MYTHS OF OUR TIME

The process of myth-making continues to affect people and ways of thinking in modern societies, even though we may not recognize it. Most Western societies, for instance, have an unshakable faith in the "truth" as represented by science, technology, and economic growth. Their heroes are the outstanding discoverers and inventors: people who have made those societies what they are proud to be.

Many famous people of recent times were very different from their mythical portrayals. The real lawman Wyatt Earp (1848–1929), for example, was a gambler, a horse thief, and a swindler.

The mythical truth

But myths are more powerful — and simpler — than the unvarnished and complicated historical reality. Myths represent a different kind of truth. The wild West of legend reflected values that for generations many Americans took as their own. What really happened in that era was less important than what it represented in mythical terms. Perhaps we humans find it necessary to invent a mythical past to make sense of the complex world around us.

HIAWATHA— HE MAKES RIVERS

Few lives better illustrate how legends grow up around remarkable individuals than that of the visionary Iroquois chieftain Hiawatha.

Legendary hero
This illustration of an Iroquois warrior by American artist George Catlin (1796–1872) dates from about 1830, by which time the Hiawatha legend had become complex and widespread.

THE LARGE IROQUOIS CONFEDERACY was originally divided into five warring tribes, or Nations — Mohawks, Oneidas, Senecas, Onondagas, and Cayugas. According to archeological evidence, the real Hiawatha (the name means "he makes rivers") lived during the late 16th century. Some legends relate that he was born into the Mohawk tribe. Later, when the Mohawks rejected his attempts to unite the Iroquois people, he fled their lands and was adopted by the Onondagas. Other traditions reverse the story, having him born into the Onondagas, later to take refuge among the Mohawks.

Visionary statesman
No one disputes, however, that Hiawatha was a visionary statesman who recognized that the Iroquois should unite to defend their common interests. He dreamed of a *Kayanerenh Kowa*, a Grand Council, which would resolve problems among the Five Nations and be a deterrent to their common enemies. The greatest obstacle to the realization of his vision was Atotarho, the formidable chief of the Onondagas, who blocked all Hiawatha's attempts to replace warfare with cooperation.

Strategic changes
After repeatedly being thwarted in achieving his dream by Atotarho at general councils of the Five Nations, Hiawatha changed strategy and began to create the alliance one step at a time. First, he approached the Oneidas, who finally allied themselves with him; next, the Cayugas joined the council.

In the meantime, overtures to Atotarho continued to be rebuffed. At this point, with consummate diplomacy, Hiawatha invited the great warrior chief to head the alliance. According to some

> Hiawatha dreamed of a Grand Council which would resolve problems among the Five Nations and provide a mighty deterrent to their common enemies.

Happy couple
Based on Longfellow's poem, this image of Hiawatha and his bride is from an early 20th-century book illustration by Innes Fripp.

accounts, Atotarho accepted, and persuaded the Senecas to complete the confederation. Other reports say that Atotarho joined the Kayanerenh Kowa because he had no alternative. In revenge for his loss of face, he allegedly killed Hiawatha's daughter, Mni-haha.

However troubled its formation, the league soon included many more tribes, as the combined might of the Grand Council impressed them with the advantages of alliance. It destroyed its enemies, most notably the Hurons, ancient cousins of the Iroquois.

"Westward, westward, Hiawatha"
This 1910 illustration to Longfellow's poem shows the chief disappearing in a magic white canoe.

By the early 17th century, the Iroquois confederation controlled the land from the Great Lakes to Manhattan. At the time, the British and the French were in the middle of a long battle over North American territorial claims. The confederation took the British side, so the French supported the Hurons, incurring the wrath of their Iroquois enemies. The conflict was not resolved

for 150 years, but the Iroquois–British alliance was instrumental in causing the French retreat from the Americas. Sadly, the British soon brushed aside the Iroquois, partly out of fear but also in the names of progress and Christianity.

Growth of a legend
In a society without written records, a figure as charismatic as Hiawatha was bound to become the subject of legend. And so it proved.

In 19th-century folklore, he was transformed from the unifier of the Iroquois into the human embodiment of *Tarenyawagon*, the divine "Upholder of the Heavens." In a legendary version of history, Hiawatha both founded each tribe and led it to its appointed territory. In addition, he also dispensed the arts of civilization and the magic by which humankind overcame the forces of hostile nature.

As Tarenyawagon, Hiawatha bestowed various gifts on the tribes: skill in archery to the Mohawks, fleetness of foot to the Senecas, navigation to the Cayugas, lawmaking to the Onondagas, weaponry and basket making to the Oneidas. To all he gave survival skills — hunting, farming, and healing — plus a love of the arts.

Giver of wisdom
The legend recounted that the tribes prospered until hunters (probably based on the Hurons) attacked from the north. On Hiawatha's orders, the Nations — not yet united — gathered by the Salt Lake. With his daughter, Mni-haha, he came to them through the air in his magic canoe.

After he greeted them, the legend continues, a vast white bird descended and bore Mni-haha away. Hiawatha then spoke, advising the Nations to join forces against the enemy. Picking up five of the bird's feathers, he gave the Five Nations the name Iroquois.

The following day, the chiefs agreed to unite and begged Hiawatha to lead them. He refused, and with a few final words of wisdom, departed into the sky forever.

Henry W. Longfellow

THE THIRD MAN
When Henry W. Longfellow (1807–82) published his epic poem *The Song of Hiawatha* in 1855, it was an immediate success. Since then, it has given generations of readers the impression that they have gained some sense of the life of the American Indians before the coming of the white man, in what is now the northeastern part of North America.

Unreliable information
However, Longfellow's Hiawatha has nothing to do with either the Hiawatha of historical fact or his legendary persona as found in Iroquois tradition.

Longfellow is known to have used H. R. Schoolcraft's *Algic Researches* (1839) as his source material, but it is apparent that Schoolcraft confused Hiawatha in many ways with the Algonquin divinity Manabozho. In history and in the Iroquois tradition Mni-haha was always Hiawatha's daughter. But, in another major departure, Longfellow altered her name slightly, to Minihaha, and made her Hiawatha's wife.

ONCE AND FUTURE KINGS

Both the Ethiopian emperor Haile Selassie and the American rock star Elvis Presley have inspired legends suggesting that they did not die but are "waiting" to return. Similar beliefs have sprung up around charismatic figures throughout the ages.

"*I*-AND-I ARE THE RIGHTEOUS CHILDREN, we are the seeds and servants of his majesty. We listen to the voice from the throne and we're marching.... Selassie-I, Rastafari Selassie-I don't look backward, for there's a kingdom, there's a land that has been promised and we're sure of it, God must come."

This was Jamaican musician Black Kush's summary of his Rastafarian faith. Rastafarians claim that black people are the descendants of the Israelites. To them, Ethiopia is heaven and the Promised Land. Rastafarians habitually refer to themselves as "I-and-I," which means both the self and the God who dwells within the self.

The living God
The Rastafarian movement originated in Jamaica following the coronation in 1930 of Prince Ras Tafari as Haile Selassie I, emperor of Ethiopia. Rastafarians believe that Haile Selassie was the living God and the returned Jesus. This belief remained unshaken by the death of the Ethiopian emperor in 1975. Many Rastafarians think that Haile Selassie has simply dropped out of sight and that he will indeed return one day to lead his people to freedom.

No less controversial beliefs have also surfaced concerning Elvis Presley since his death at the age of 42, in August 1977. There are two basic strands to the "Elvis lives" legend. One is that Elvis did not die, but assumed another identity. The other is that Elvis did die, but still walks the earth as a ghost or in a more physical form as a kind of resurrected being. Both beliefs hinge on the hundreds of reports of "Elvis sightings" that are collected by obsessional Presley fans.

Graves with no bodies
Many of those who continue to claim that Elvis Presley did not die, maintain that there are no bodies in the graves of his family at

The emperor of Ethiopia
At his coronation in 1930 Haile Selassie also took the titles King of Kings and Lord of Lords, Conquering Lion of the Tribe of Judah, Elect of God, and Light of the World.

Immortalized in stone
This statue of the young Elvis stands in the grounds of Graceland, his home in Memphis.

Graceland, the Memphis mansion that was his home. A typical Elvis sighting was reported by two Presley fans who, on the 10th anniversary of his death, were walking in the Memphis cemetery where Presley's mother had first been buried. Ted Harrison records their encounter in his 1992 book on the Elvis cult, *Elvis People*: "They saw a man in a cap with his eyes shielded by dark glasses. As they passed by they both recognized him as Elvis." Some fans have even claimed that on similar occasions Presley has spoken to them and admitted his identity.

Presley impersonators

There is little doubt that at least some of these reports stem from sightings of the hundreds of Presley impersonators who, as both professionals and amateurs, look like him, dress like him, and perform his music. But still the "Elvis lives" legend flourishes. Many fans are convinced that he will come out of hiding and resume a public life, and some have even set a date for this return.

The Haile Selassie and Elvis examples are firmly rooted in the 20th century. But they also cast a fascinating light on the legend of an ancient king who, it is said, would return from a centuries-long sleep to save his people at a moment of supreme danger — King Arthur.

Imaginary figure

The exact identity of the historical King Arthur and the location of his court at Camelot have long been a mystery. Some researchers place him — more by guesswork than hard evidence — as a British mercenary leader in the fifth century, with a major power base in southwest England. Many others have denied his actual existence, preferring to think of him as a purely imaginary figure. Nevertheless the legend of King Arthur's return was so powerful in the Middle Ages that it became a focus for Welsh resistance to the "foreign" Norman kings of England.

The legends of Haile Selassie and Elvis Presley repeat this theme of return after death — and they were real people. Could this lend some support to the possibility that King Arthur was also a real person, with such a powerful personality and so vital a political role that his death could not easily be accepted by his followers?

Elvis's tomb?
One piece of "evidence" fans use to support the theory that Elvis's body is not in his tomb, is the apparent misspelling of Presley's middle name (Aaron instead of Aron) on his tombstone. Another is the fact that the grave is aligned north-to-south, not east-to-west as in most Christian graveyards.

Was King Arthur also a real person, with such a powerful personality and so vital a political role that his death could not easily be accepted by his followers?

King Arthur's grave?
The return of King Arthur was so passionately awaited by 12th-century Bretons and Welsh that the resulting political agitation may have prompted the English king Henry II to instigate the "discovery" of King Arthur's grave at Glastonbury in 1191.

CHAPTER TWO

PUZZLES OF THE PYRAMIDS

Stones piled on stones, that is all the pyramids are — and yet what stones! By day or night, the sheer height and bulk of the Great Pyramid of King Khufu have held visitors in awe for 45 centuries.

The Great Pyramid of King Khufu (often known by his Greek name, Cheops) is the largest of all the pyramids. It is the right-hand one of the three that are seen raised up on the edge of the desert plateau at Giza as travelers — or pilgrims — cross the Nile from Cairo. It once stood about 480 feet high, and even now, though stripped of the finer-grained casing stones that were removed and taken off to build medieval

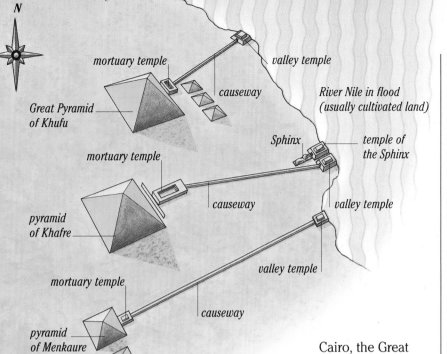

N

mortuary temple

Great Pyramid of Khufu

valley temple

causeway

River Nile in flood (usually cultivated land)

Sphinx

temple of the Sphinx

mortuary temple

pyramid of Khafre

causeway

valley temple

valley temple

mortuary temple

causeway

pyramid of Menkaure

small pyramids

The Giza pyramids viewed from the south

Pyramids galore
The pyramids of Giza viewed from the south. In the fore-ground, in front of the pyramid of Menkaure, stand three subsidiary pyramids, which were apparently used for the burial of King Menkaure's queens and princesses. Behind Menkaure's pyramid stand those of Khafre and Khufu, respectively. From this vantage point, the effects of perspective make Khafre's pyramid look taller than Khufu's Great Pyramid. This is because it stands on higher ground and has steeper sides than that of Khufu.

Cairo, the Great Pyramid of Khufu at Giza reaches up 450 feet. Beside it the slightly smaller pyramid of Khafre (Chephren in Greek) stands at just over 448 feet. By comparison, the Washington Monument stands 555 feet tall.

The awe inspired by the pyramids' size is soon followed by wonder at the technical achievements they represent. The pyramids at Giza date back almost to the dawn of civilization itself, to the early days of the Egyptian Old Kingdom, some 2,500 years before Christ's birth. Khufu's Great Pyramid contains roughly

2 1/2 million blocks of limestone, most weighing between 2 1/2 and 5 tons. The total adds up to about 20 times the weight of New York's Empire State Building. High within the pyramid runs the Grand Gallery, a sloping corridor 156 feet long and 28 feet high, which leads in turn to the King's Chamber, 34 feet long and 19 feet high, built of huge, well-finished, and finely jointed granite blocks brought down the Nile from Aswan.

Even when the pyramid's awesome size and structure have been absorbed, many questions remain unanswered. Why were these vast edifices built? What were they intended for? How were they built? Since the ancient Egyptians have left us no records, we have to rely on informed guesswork for most answers.

Luxurious afterlife

Supporting all theories about the building of the pyramids is the strong belief that we feel the Egyptians had in an afterlife — an afterlife visualized much as an extension of an ideal life on earth. For kings the implications were grandiose: a luxurious existence in the companion-ship of the eternal gods.

Even in the earliest Egyptian burials, from about 4000 B.C., each body, laid in an oval pit dug out of agriculturally worthless desert land, wore fine clothing and had beside it an array of pots and

tools. As time went by, burials became more elaborate, with chambered tombs holding funerary goods such as model houses and decorated vases.

Tombs of the kings

By the beginning of the Early Dynastic Period, about 3000 B.C., the royal tombs of Egypt were displaying more and more splendor. The two lands, of Upper Egypt spread along the Nile and Lower Egypt covering the Nile Delta, had become one, with a capital at Memphis, to the southwest, close to the site of present-day Cairo. These early kings built their main tombs at Sâqqara on the edge of the steep desert escarpment to the west of their new capital, turning their sight toward the setting sun.

At first these royal tombs, called mastabas, appeared very similar to the royal palace itself, single-story, mud-brick buildings, divided into storage chambers, set above a burial chamber and surrounded by the graves of other members of the royal household. With passing time and the realization that robbers might break in and steal the

> ## The Step Pyramid remains a major presence, glowing pinkly in the dawn, standing out white against the blue expanse of daytime sky.

---

contents, the burial chamber was driven deeper into the rock while the super-structure became a solid mass, with, beside it, a small temple where the living could make offerings to the dead.

The jump from mastaba to pyramid came about 2700 B.C. with the Step Pyramid of Djoser. King Djoser's administrator and architect, Imhotep, used stone for the first time in building a solid mastaba. Then, realizing the possibilities of the material, he added further layers, making six steps, more than 200 feet high on a base about 410 by 360 feet. The structure remains a major presence, glowing pinkly in the dawn, standing out white against the

clear blue expanse of daytime sky, and looming black before the fiery reds and yellows of the setting sun.

Succeeding kings built imitations, until one took the next step, raising a pyramid at Meidum, 22 miles to the south of Sâqqara, then packing the sides with fine-grained limestone to make the first of the true, smooth-faced pyramids. More followed, including one called the Bent Pyramid, because the angle of the slope changed about halfway up. The builders, presumably, were still coming to terms with the techniques used later for the giant monuments of Giza.

Royal builders

All this building leads up to that greatest achievement of all, the three pyramids at Giza built by kings Khufu, Khafre, and Menkaure (Mycerinus in Greek) over the period 2600 to 2500 B.C.

For a further 600 to 700 years, although interrupted by periods of political upheaval, Egyptian kings continued to build pyramids, but never again were they as large or as finely constructed as those at Giza. In many cases the core of these later pyramids was made up of smallish stones bonded roughly together with Nile mud, or even of mud bricks. Once the facing stones were stripped off by later builders, the core crumbled.

Altogether the Egyptian kings built about 35 major pyramids, most of them spread along the 50-mile stretch of the west bank of the Nile, south of Cairo. Just one or two, such as the pyramid above the temple of Mentuhotep II, were placed far to the south near Thebes, now Luxor.

Most of the kings of the Old Kingdom (which lasted from about 2700 to 2200 B.C.), built pyramids. So did those of the Middle Kingdom, reestablished (after a period of political disunity), from 2050 to 1800 B.C. Even during the following period of upheaval, with foreign rulers moving into the Nile Delta, some kings with local power still built pyramids. The custom ended with the first kings of the New Kingdom (which probably lasted from about 1550 to 1050 B.C.). During the New Kingdom, Egypt reached the highest point of its power and prosperity, but kings such as Tutankhamen, who ruled about 1350 B.C., put their hopes for the afterlife into sepulchral vaults dug deep into the bedrock of the Valley of the Kings near Thebes.

Missing body

Obviously the royal pyramids were funerary monuments, but it is not always clear that each one has an actual tomb. For example, although the Great Pyramid contained a sarcophagus it is not known whether it ever contained King Khufu's corpse. Some kings built more than one pyramid, and several built additional tombs in southern Egypt, at Abydos, presumably as homes for their spirits when visiting the festivals celebrating the god Osiris.

Complex deterrent

Khufu's Great Pyramid is the only one with corridors and chambers high within the structure itself. Most of the earlier pyramids have a burial chamber beneath the center of the pyramid reached directly by a passage mostly tunneled through the base rock. Later on these passages became more complex, with false turnings and mechanisms to lower slabs of stone in order to block them off. However, over the decades, thieves invariably found their way in to steal whatever might have been buried.

Perhaps the move from burial beneath a pyramid to burial within an almost unmarked rock-cut tomb was effected in the hope of avoiding the attentions of tomb robbers. A pyramid itself was a fairly obvious marker that something worthwhile might be dug up. The architect of the first royal burial in the Valley of the Kings, that of Thutmose I, who reigned about 1500 B.C., left an inscription saying that he had carried out the construction in secret.

Changing attitudes

It is possible that some shift in religious symbolism occurred as the kings of the New Kingdom gave greater prominence to the priests of the god Amon, whose temples congregated around Thebes. The pyramid shape, however, did retain some significance, because private tombs incorporating a hollow, brick-built pyramid continued to be built right down to Roman times.

It may just be that the potential benefits to be gained in the afterlife no longer outweighed the enormous efforts

> ## A pyramid itself was a fairly obvious marker that something worthwhile might be dug up.

and costs involved in the building of a pyramid.

There is much speculation as to how the Egyptians constructed the pyramids; how they aligned them north and south and measured off the sides. The Great Pyramid lines up within one-tenth of a degree of true north. The

Awesome labyrinth

Khufu's Great Pyramid contains a complicated series of ramps, passages, and galleries, as well as three burial chambers. The third chamber is the highest, and it contained Khufu's empty stone sarcophagus. Passages to the chamber were originally blocked by huge stone slabs to deter tomb robbers. This illustration by Luigi Mayer, from Sir Robert Ainslie's Views of Egypt, *published at the beginning of the 19th century, shows the Grand Gallery.*

King Khufu

An ivory statuette of the king responsible for building the Great Pyramid at Giza.

lengths of the sides, at just over 756 feet, differ by less than eight inches.

In the 19th century a number of scientists and amateurs became fascinated by the mysteries of the pyramids. There was much speculation, some of it quite out of control, as to how and why the pyramids had been built. Some people suggested that the Egyptians took observations from the stars. Others pointed out that the Egyptian religion centered on the sun, and that tracking the shadow cast by an upright pole on appropriate days of the year could have pinpointed true north.

Bible in stone

Others took up and extended the idea of the Great Pyramid as "the Bible in stone," promising dates for the Second Coming and for the ending of false religions. Some went in for numerology, claiming that the number five runs through all aspects of the construction. Some referred to links with Freemasonry — promising that Freemasons would one day repair Khufu's tomb. Some wondered if it was divine inspiration that put the Great Pyramid on the reverse of the Great Seal of the United States, which is printed on the dollar bill.

People have claimed that the pyramid shape itself has power. Devotees of pyramid-power have reportedly shown to their own satisfaction that razor blades regain sharpness if left under a pyramid-shaped container, that prayer becomes more effective, psychic phenomena stronger, and so on.

A French ironmonger, Antoine Bovis, was the first to make such claims, between the two World Wars. Bovis, who also ran a business selling divinatory pendulums and the like, visited the Great Pyramid and noticed that the bodies of animals that had climbed into the King's Chamber and died there appeared to be perfectly preserved. Experiments with a model pyramid allegedly produced the same effect.

Karl Drbal, a Czechoslovakian radio technician, reasoned that this regenerative effect on animals would also apply to other materials. In 1959, after a 10-year struggle, he acquired a patent for a "Pharaonic Shaving Device." It consisted of a cardboard model of the Great Pyramid, under which he would keep a razor blade. Such was the alleged regenerative power of the device that Drbal claimed he had achieved more than 100 shaves from one blade.

What the ancient Egyptians intended by building these pyramid shapes is itself still to be discovered. One of the earliest fragments of Egyptian writing may refer to the Step Pyramid when it says, "A staircase to heaven is laid for him that he may ascend it to the sky." True pyramids, such as the Great Pyramid, may, in their angularity, have reminded onlookers of the rays of the sun striking down to welcome the newly dead.

Mountainous monument

Unlike the ziggurats, the pyramid-shaped temple towers of Mesopotamia that functioned as artificial mountains and as platforms for astronomical observations, the Egyptian pyramids were pure monuments. Yet perhaps they did symbolize a mountain of sorts, the primeval mound that first emerged from the waters of chaos and on which the Egyptian god Aton stood as he created the universe. Or maybe the pyramids developed from the simple heap of sand and gravel that marked and protected the earliest burials.

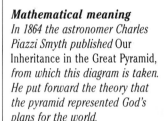

Mathematical meaning
In 1864 the astronomer Charles Piazzi Smyth published Our Inheritance in the Great Pyramid, *from which this diagram is taken. He put forward the theory that the pyramid represented God's plans for the world.*

SPECULATIVE MEASUREMENTS
In 1864 the Astronomer Royal for Scotland, Charles Piazzi Smyth, claimed that the Great Pyramid was based on the most natural measurement, the Pyramid inch, which equalled 1.00099 English inches. He confidently claimed that this discovery would put the despicable metric system to rout.

Designs for the world
Taking his experiments one step further, but using other people's measurements, Piazzi Smyth computed the ratio of the height of the Great Pyramid to twice its base, pointing out triumphantly that it matched the value for *pi,* the ratio of the circumference of a circle to twice its radius.

Later he adopted a theory that the internal layout of the pyramid represented a condensed history of the world. For example, he predicted the Second Coming of Christ sometime in the 1880's.

The reverse of a dollar bill

PYRAMID BUILDING

How did a civilization that had not yet discovered the wheel build an immense structure such as the Great Pyramid?

No photograph can convey the awe-inspiring scale of the pyramids. In the early 19th century, surveyors of the French emperor Napoleon calculated that the stones that make up the three pyramids at Giza would build a wall around France 10 feet high and more than 3 feet thick.

Some speculators have rashly suggested that only a master race of extraterrestrial aliens could have managed such an engineering miracle. But apart from the scale of the job, the building of the pyramids would present no major difficulties to a civilization that had metal tools, skilled workmen, and an unlimited supply

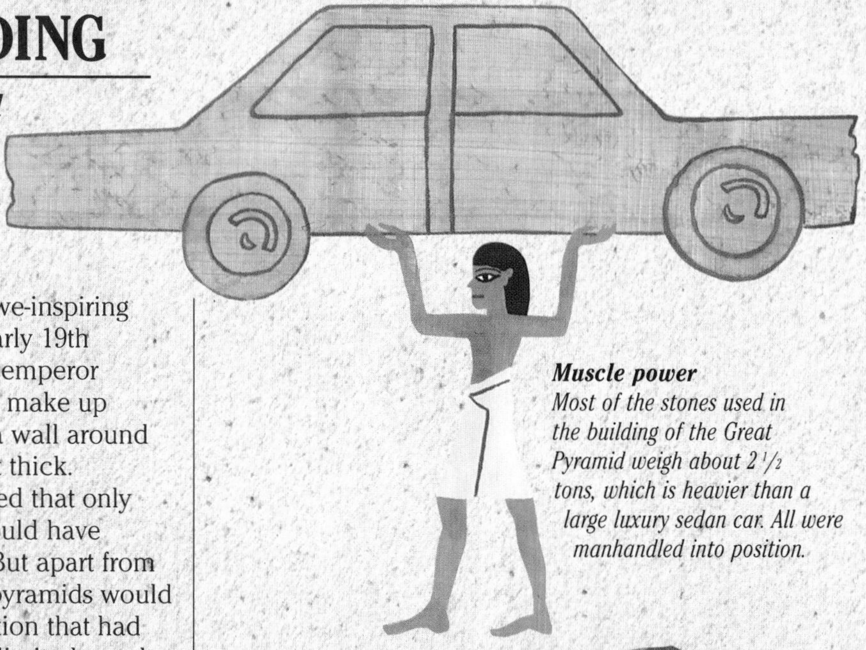

Muscle power
Most of the stones used in the building of the Great Pyramid weigh about 2 ¹/₂ tons, which is heavier than a large luxury sedan car. All were manhandled into position.

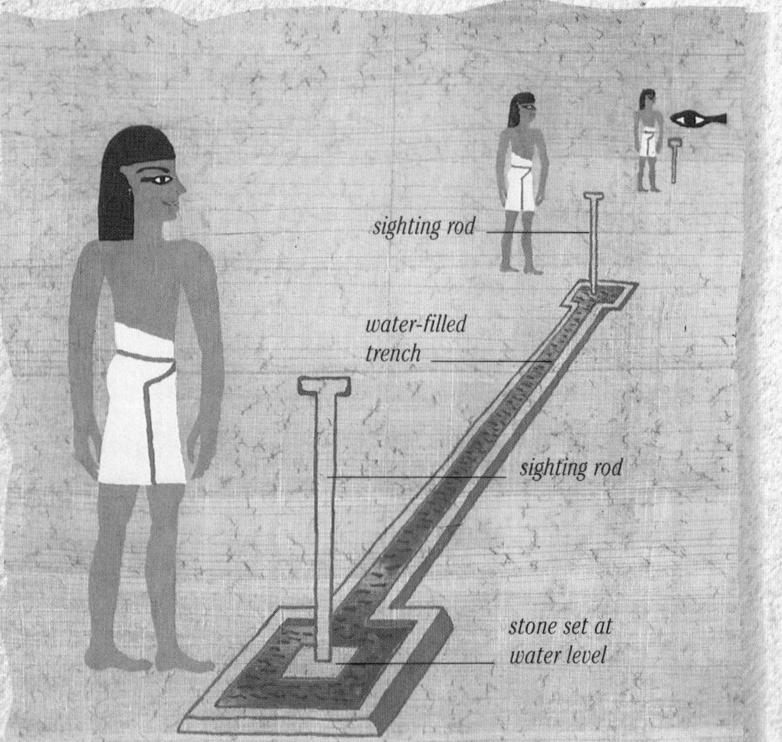

sighting rod

water-filled trench

sighting rod

stone set at water level

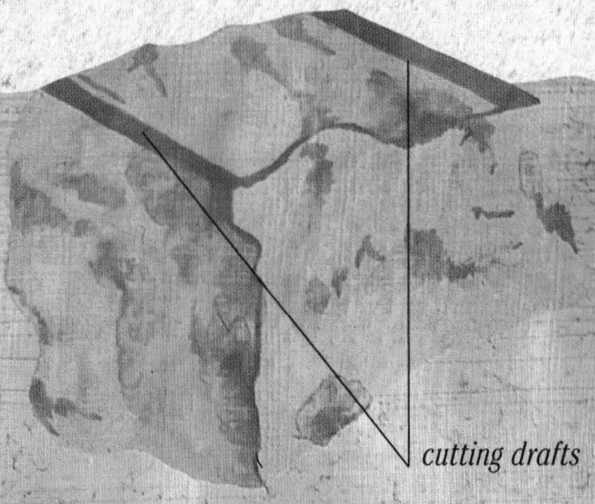

Cutting the blocks
Using copper chisels and saws, the ancient Egyptians cut limestone blocks out of the quarries near the pyramid site. Flat channels called drafts were cut at each end of the block, and a straight-edge was laid along each end to see whether the drafts were parallel. When the excess stone was chipped away and the surface was flat, a square was inscribed on the surface. To make a cube, this square was repeated on the other faces of the stone by duplicating its diagonal length.

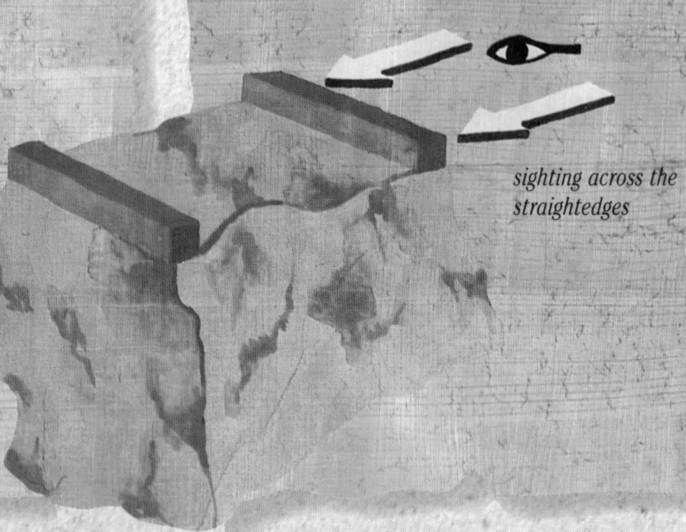

cutting drafts

sighting across the straightedges

Preparing the site
The surveyors started by orienting the site to the north, based on their observations of the sun and stars. Then they dug a shallow, water-filled trench along one side of the site. Sighting rods of equal length were then set up on stones set at the water level. Sighting along these rods to other rods showed whether the ground was high or low. The pyramid had to be built on base rock, so the whole site (13 acres) had to be leveled to the lowest point.

of limestone. The ancient Egyptians had all these, plus a huge labor force.

Transporting and lifting the blocks up the sides of the pyramid were the main problems. The only ancient account of how this task was done refers to the Great Pyramid, and is from *The Histories* of Herodotus, the Greek historian:

"The method employed was to build it in steps, or, as some call them, tiers or terraces. When the base was complete, the blocks for the first tier above it were

> # The building of the pyramids would present no major difficulties to a civilization that had metal tools, skilled work-men, and an unlimited supply of limestone.

lifted from ground level by contrivances made of short timbers; on this first tier there was another, which raised the blocks a stage higher, then yet another, which raised them higher still. Each tier or story, had its set of levers, or it may be that they used the same one, which, being easy to carry, they shifted up from stage to stage as soon as its load was dropped into place. Both methods were mentioned, so I give them both here. The finishing-off of the pyramid was begun at the top and continued down-wards, ending with the lowest parts nearest to the ground."

Moving the blocks

The blocks of stone were probably transported to the site on wooden rollers or on sledges, sliding along on a mix of water and mud or slaked lime. How the blocks themselves were actually raised into place is still a mystery. The idea that they were eased up a straight ramp has been discounted. Any such ramp would have had a volume, in the final stages, three times that of the pyramid itself.

moving the block on rollers

levering the block sideways

inserting wooden blocks

levering the block up

New theory

In How the Pyramids Were Built *(1989), the author and master builder Peter Hodges suggested that the builders used simple metal-reinforced wooden levers to raise the blocks stage by stage, jamming in blocks of wood below them after each lift. This theory was tested and found to be feasible in practice. With skilled teams of four men to each 2 1/2-ton block, working on three of the pyramid's faces at once, Hodges reckoned that a work force of 1,000 men could have lifted the blocks into position.*

Scale of the problem

The Great Pyramid was built out of approximately 2 1/2 million limestone blocks, most of which measured 4 feet x 4 feet x 2 1/2 feet and weighed about 2 1/2 tons each. (This makes a total weight more than 20 times that of the Empire State Building.) The blocks were laid in about 200 level courses to make up the core of the pyramid.

The Great Pyramid was about 480 feet high when built (though it has lost some height since then through erosion). It dwarfs the Statue of Liberty (305 feet from foundation to torch). The Great Pyramid is 756 feet square at the base. For comparison, a Boeing 747 jumbo jet is 232 feet long. The pyramid's sides are pitched at an angle of 52 degrees.

"Facing" the pyramid
The Great Pyramid originally had smooth sides, before these stones were stripped off in the 13th century. Large four-ton blocks of white limestone were used for the outer layer. They may have been dressed before being raised and set in place (left). But they would have provided a better seal if they were set in place as blocks and then trimmed (far left).

trim off   fill in

of probably between 4,000 and 10,000 applied themselves to the more skilled tasks of shaping stones and planning how to deliver them to the right place and in the right sequence.

All this effort must have drained the country's resources. But at this time, about 2600 B.C., the kingdoms of Upper and Lower Egypt had been united for about 600 years. Khufu, the second pharaoh of the Fourth Dynasty, ruled a powerful and extensive country. It seems that the organization that went into supervising the work, arranging for so many people to be fed and housed,

But this account was written some 2,000 years after the pyramids were built, and may be just a story told by local people.

Construction of the pyramid itself probably stretched out over 20 or 30 years, much of the king's reign, and on top of that task came the building of the surrounding pavement and enclosure wall, a mortuary temple beside the pyramid, and another temple on the edge of the valley, linked to the mortuary temple by a 1,650-foot causeway.

High-quality stone
Stone for much of the pyramid's core was quarried from the plateau itself, but the white facing blocks had to be ferried across the river. Most theories about the building of the pyramids suggest that the stones were transported during the months when the silt-laden Nile flooded the valley fields and little agricultural work could be done. Herodotus said that 100,000 men worked on hauling stones. A year-round force

> ### "The finishing-off of the pyramid was begun at the top and continued downwards, ending with the lowest parts nearest the ground."
>
> **Herodotus**

and collecting the taxes that made it all possible, was well within the power of the pharaoh. And such a huge building project, while serving to glorify the king's name, may have had an ulterior motive. It may have been seen as a useful ploy to forge a single state out of what was still a group of provinces.

King's Chamber
ventilation shaft
Grand Gallery
ascending passage
Queen's Chamber
descending passage

Inside the pyramid
The Great Pyramid contains a complex arrangement of shafts, passages, and galleries. These make use of even larger stones, up to 50-ton blocks of granite, shipped down the Nile from Aswan, 450 miles away. The internal spaces were apparently built as the pyramid slowly rose, level by level. A huge staircase may have been left on one side of the pyramid to make it easier to lift these larger stones to their positions.

King's Chamber
giant staircase

BUILDING A PYRAMID TODAY

A large international construction firm was asked to produce a tender for the job of building the Great Pyramid.

EVEN WITH today's technology, the building of the Great Pyramid is an overwhelming project. At the request of the editors, an international construction firm estimated a budget of US$300 million, a four-year schedule, and a work force of 3,000, working day and night.

The main differences in ancient and modern construction techniques are those of scale. With trucks that can carry 10 x 2 1/2-ton blocks at once and a giant conveyor belt and a hoist to lift them up the sides of the pyramid, much time could be saved. Another difference is that the pyramid would be built in 48-foot "steps," to allow space for the heavy machinery to be mounted and to operate.

PYRAMID PROJECT
(major parameters)
TOTALS
project time   48 months
"   cost   US $300 million
"   man hours   15 million
construction = 6 days per week
maintenance = 1 day per week
PROJECT WORK WEEK   3 hours per shift
  3 shifts per day
Peak work force   1,000 man per shift
x 3 shifts = 3,000 man

NEW PYRAMID COST BREAKDOWN	US$M
Engineering and design	20.0
Quarries/wharf – site development	2.5
Haul roads – construction	18.0
Barges/tugs	6.0
Trucks (18)	5.5
Drivers/crew/wharf	6.0
Core stone quarry – labor/materials	15.0
Surface stone quarry – labor/materials	5.0
Camps – construction	33.0
Camps – operating costs	23.0
Foundation preparations	5.0
Land acquisition	30.0
Unloading/loading equipment	10.0
Conveyor	7.0
Material/man hoist	3.0
Labor/supervision	50.0
Clean-up/landscaping	10.0
Consumables	20.0
Subtotal	269.0
Contingency	31.0
GRAND TOTAL (US$ millions)	300.0

Lifting the blocks
The ordinary blocks would be lifted up the sides of the pyramid by a chain conveyor at the rate of one every 10 seconds. They could then be moved into position by a fleet of forklift-type trucks.

Heavy hoist
The large granite blocks (up to 50 tons) for the King's Chamber would be lifted into position on a special hoist platform, powered by a winch on the ground. They could then be dropped into position by a crane.

Laying the blocks
Modern quarrying techniques would speed up the production of the stone blocks, but they would not be trimmed with the accuracy the Egyptians achieved. Instead, they would be laid in their rough-quarried state and the layers leveled with gravel. Four types of machines would be used (below, left to right): a front-end loader, a dump truck, a grader, and a roller.

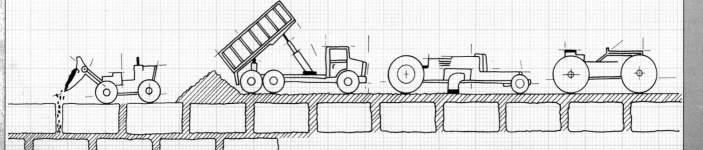

BACK TO THE FUTURE

In the late 1960's the county council in Northampton, England, decided to centralize its resources in one building. In July 1971, with this idea in mind, it launched a competition, with a £7,000 first prize, to find the best design. The council stipulated that the building should cost no more than £5 million to construct and should be completed by 1978.

A panel of council leaders and eminent architects had to choose from more than 200 entries. Out of nine finalists the panel decided on a pyramidal structure designed by Jeremy and Fenella Dixon and

MODERN PYRAMIDS

Pyramids as tombs, as monuments, as museums, as office blocks, and as homes. The ancient shape, with its supernatural overtones, continues to inspire modern architects and to entertain and intrigue present-day observers.

Building blocks
The Trans American office block in San Francisco, California.

The pyramid that never was
A model of the prizewinning design for Northampton council's municipal building.

Edward Jones. These innovative architects pointed out the advantages of their remarkable design: "It is a sensible shape for keeping the water out. It's an economical shape. It's a hierarchical shape, with large open plan areas at the base rising to the council chamber and chief executive's offices at the top."

Abandoned design

However, some council members were not taken with the futuristic concept. They pointed out that "a giant glass pyramid is particularly unsuitable for the rolling land-scape of Northamptonshire." The design was eventually abandoned.

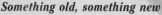

Something old, something new
The pyramid that forms the main entrance to the Louvre in Paris consists of 666 panes of glass attached to a chassis of steel tubes. Designed by Chinese-born American architect Ieoh Ming Pei, the pyramid was considered highly controversial when it first opened to the public in 1989.

Eccentric squire

An eccentric English member of parliament, Squire Mad Jack Fuller, was obviously taken with pyramids — he decided that he wished to be buried in one. Mad Jack had his pyramid built in the cemetery of the Church of St. Thomas à Becket in Brightling, Sussex. Local legend has it that, following his death in 1834, he was entombed in the center of the pyramid, sitting in an iron chair, fully dressed, and with a bottle of port and a roast chicken in front of him, so that he could wait in comfort for the Resurrection.

Mad Jack Fuller's final resting place

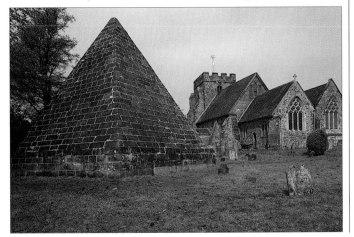

Marble mausoleum

Mary B. Hecht was a football-loving American millionairess who lived life to its fullest. And she was just as unique when it came to her death. She left instructions that she wished to be buried in "a mausoleum of pink marble, formed in the shape of a pyramid with the front to be decorated with an appropriate copy of the Egyptian Sphinx." Following her death in March 1982 it took a year to complete the tomb, at a cost of $147,000. The nine-foot-high pyramid is made of rose marble from Tate, Georgia, and the 1.2-ton white marble sphinx that stands before it was sculpted in Carrara, Italy. More than 30 guests sipped champagne when Mary Hecht's funeral was finally held in April 1983 at the Woodlawn Park Cemetery, Miami.

Mary B. Hecht's mausoleum

LIVING IN A PYRAMID

A visitor to the town of Wadsworth, Illinois, 45 minutes' drive north of Chicago, may be surprised to stumble across a landscape straight out of ancient Egypt. On a 10-acre plot of land stands a real pyramid, complete with palm trees, a moat, a 28-foot statue of the pharaoh Ramses II, and a line of sphinxes.

This is the home of James Onan. The pyramid is a one-ninth scale model of the Great Pyramid of Khufu at Giza. Onan started the five-story building in 1974 and completed it 12 years later in 1986.

No expense spared

Onan has opened his home to the public, who have flocked in their thousands to see the wonder of a modern pyramid in Illinois. The pyramid is designed to be a conventional family home, and so it is not an exact replica of the Great Pyramid. However, Onan has spared no expense in his attempt to re-create the splendor of the pharaohs. In place of the limestone facing blocks that originally covered the Great Pyramid, his contemporary pyramid is coated with tissue-thin 24-carat gold plating.

The American pharaoh

James Onan built a gilded family home in Wadsworth, Illinois (above). The house sits on an island that is surrounded by a 24-foot-deep spring-fed moat (left).

THE INSCRUTABLE SPHINX

No one knows exactly when it was built or why, but the enigmatic Egyptian Sphinx leaves a remarkable, and lasting, memory in the minds of everybody who visits it.

ARAB PHYSICIAN AND WRITER Abd al Latif, who traveled through Egypt about A.D. 1200, was asked what had most impressed him. He answered without hesitation: "The head of the Sphinx." He was astonished that the sculptors who created the Sphinx had managed to match the proportions of the human face so exactly on such a large scale, conveying a sense of grace and beauty to the extent that the onlooker might fancy it breaking into a smile.

When Abd al Latif saw it, the Sphinx was already nearly 4,000 years old. It is a vast, human-headed lion, about 240 feet long, 66 feet high, and 13 feet wide. It sits in a hollow to the east of the pyramid of King Khafre, the middle one of the three pyramids of Giza. Carved from a rock outcrop, the Sphinx may originally have been enclosed in limestone blocks, or coated with plaster, and brightly painted.

Royal model

The Sphinx wears the royal headdress and is thought to be modeled on the face of Khafre himself. Most experts put its construction at about 2600 to 2500 B.C., although some investigators, citing the erosions of the Sphinx's body, have suggested a date at least 500 to 1,000 years earlier. The later date adds weight to the idea that the hollow within which the Sphinx sits was a quarry that provided stone for Khafre's pyramid.

Even in ancient Egyptian times the Sphinx excited admiration. Later

Regal stature
The Sphinx at Giza has a lion's body and a king's head. The ancient Egyptians thought that the lion's strength reflected the monarch's great power. They also believed the lion was a creature of the sun god Re and that using the lion's body with the king's head emphasized the king's role as son of the sun god.

generations believed it to represent the god Harmachis. One pharaoh, Thutmose IV, who ruled about 1400 B.C., made use of the Sphinx's prestige in consolidating his own power. He had a carved slab placed in front of the Sphinx explaining the story of how he fell asleep while hunting and how the god promised him the throne of Egypt if he cleared away the sand that covered the Sphinx. Thutmose IV did as he was told — the brick wall he built to hold back the sand still exists — and claimed divine backing in taking the throne.

Secret passages

Thutmose IV's slab features in some of the myths that grew up around the Sphinx in medieval and later times. There are some who hold that the slab conceals a door that leads to an underground complex of halls and corridors known only to priestly initiates. Others believe that an entrance under the Sphinx itself leads to a passage running

> Some believe that an entrance under the Sphinx itself leads to a passage running up and into the Great Pyramid of Khufu, the largest of the pyramids at Giza.

Thutmose IV
In about 1400 B.C. Thutmose IV ordered the clearing of the sand that had built up around the Sphinx. Thutmose claimed that the god Harmachis had appeared to him in a dream, ordered him to clear the sand, and offered him the throne in return.

up and into the Great Pyramid of Khufu, the largest of the pyramids at Giza.

When Abd al Latif saw the Sphinx, it seems to have been still in its full glory. He mentions red varnish on the face, as bright as if freshly put on. The nose also was still in evidence. Some say the Sphinx lost its looks around A.D. 1300, mutilated by the Sultan Mohammed an-Nasir. Others blame the soldiers of Napoleon's expedition, lasting from 1798 to 1801, for lobbing cannon balls at it.

Whatever indignities it may have suffered, the Sphinx is still an impressive presence, particularly at the nightly *son et lumière* show put on each night for the tourists. Thus, after years of neglect, worship of a kind is still given to this enigmatic figure.

OUT OF TIME

It is generally believed by most Egyptologists that the Sphinx was built during the reign of King Khafre about 2500 B.C. But some scientists are now putting forward the theory that the Sphinx was in existence several thousand years earlier and that Khafre merely restored the gigantic monument.

A weathered look

On October 23, 1991, at a meeting of the Geological Society of America in San Diego, Boston geologist Robert Schoch presented the theory that the weathering of the Sphinx indicates a far earlier construction date than had previously been considered feasible. Schoch maintains that the Sphinx was weathered by water. The last period of heavy rainfall in Egypt was between 12,000 and 3000 B.C. From the amount of erosion present Schoch concluded that the Sphinx dates from the period 7000 to 5000 B.C.

Egyptologists responded to Schoch's claims by pointing out that the people of that time would not have been capable of creating such a monument.

CHAPTER THREE

EGYPTIAN ENIGMAS

The vast monuments, mighty tombs, and mummified burial remains of the ancient Egyptians provide many clues as to how they lived. Yet many mysteries still remain concerning one of the most sumptuous of early civilizations.

In Cairo Museum, visitors can face kings and pharaohs, major actors in the drama that was ancient Egypt. Here is Thutmose III, conqueror of Syria. There is Ramses II, slim hands peacefully crossed on his breast. Here is the priest-like Seti I, here the stout Ramses III. Any of us might look on these once mighty men and wonder at the connection that spans thousands of years.

Wonder, too, at the effort the ancient Egyptians put into preserving these bodies. Death, the ancient Egyptians hoped, would lead on to a hereafter that would be much

Natural mummy
An Egyptian corpse dating from 3200 B.C. shows the naturally desiccating effect of burial in hot, dry, desert conditions. This is the effect the ancient Egyptians later strove to produce artificially.

like life. Therefore, they reasoned, the soul of the dead person would need an earthly base from which to lead that afterlife, a base provided in part by his or her own preserved body.

In the Egyptian spiritual system each person had two souls. One, called the *ka*, was the ethereal equivalent of the corporeal body, a soul that went on after death as a shadowy version of the body that the person possessed in life. The other, called the *ba*, often depicted as a human-headed bird, was the external soul, accompanying the person through life and continuing after death.

House for the soul
So people built tombs for themselves that were much like houses, in order to provide the *ka* with somewhere to live. And they preserved the dead person's body in order to create a continuing link with the *ba*. In the earliest burials, this preservation was almost accidental. Such graves show that the body was laid in a shallow pit with a few pots and tools as grave furnishings. The hot desert sand dried out the body, which might be found hundreds of years later still lying among the clothes and tools it would need in the afterlife. As tombs became more elaborate, this natural process of desiccation could not be relied on. The body was wrapped in linen in an attempt to ensure its survival.

Soul bird
This pendant in the form of a bird, dating from about 1350 B.C., represents the ba, *or external soul.*

Broad bandages
In one burial at Sâqqara, just south of present-day Cairo, dating from about 2800 B.C., the body of a woman had been

shrouded in a complicated series of more than 16 layers of broad bandages. Later on, during the great age of pyramid building in the Old Kingdom, about 2700 to 2200 B.C., corpses were first embalmed, and then given a lifelike wrapping. Linen pads were used to create the impression of bulging muscles.

Artificial eyes
Embalmers, practicing during the New Kingdom from 1550 to 1050 B.C., became increasingly confident. They worked on the body itself, plumping it out with materials stuffed beneath the skin, even

Preserved princess
This is the face of Henttowy, mother of the pharaoh Pinudjem I. She died 3,000 years ago, at the age of 20.

setting artificial eyes in the sockets. Later still, they took short cuts, and hardly treated the body at all. Instead, they soaked the wrappings with hard-setting resins that could conceal putrefying flesh. These resins darkened to look like pitch, called *mumiya* by the Arabs, which explains how these wrapped corpses came to be called mummies.

Masks covering the face went through a similar development. The earliest

Symbol of life
Pharaohs had scarab beetles carved in stone and set in gold placed over their hearts to help them through their judgment in the afterlife.

masks were made of cartonage, layers of linen molded into shape with plaster and then painted. These masks became full-length cases and then wooden coffins. The mummy of the boy-king Tutankhamen boasted a gold mask and lay within a nest of three body-shaped coffins, the inmost one made of solid gold. Later these elaborate masks gave way to basic portraits painted on board and bound over the face.

Religious rituals

Making a mummy of a corpse took some time, probably about 70 days, every stage being marked with its own religious rituals. Soon after death, the embalmers took charge of the body. They started by

> **Making a mummy of a corpse took some time, probably about 70 days, every stage being marked with its own religious rituals.**

removing the internal organs through a slit in the side, although they left the heart in place. The man who made the first cut was, apparently, then chased away with ritual curses to remind every-one concerned that wounding a body was sacrilegious. Next, the embalmers removed the brain, perhaps after leaving it to decompose to make the job somewhat easier. It seems that the standard practice was to insert a metal hook through the nose, cut the brain apart, and wash out the fragments.

Following the removal of the organs, the embalmers next laid the corpse on a mat and covered it with natron, a drying agent. Natron, a mix of sodium carbonate and bicarbonate found in the desert, draws moisture to itself in exactly the same way that salt does in damp air. The body might be left in this way for 40 days or more. It was then washed inside and out to prepare it for a ceremony of purification, performed by priests.

Scarab beetle charm

Next came the wrapping of the corpse. First the embalmers packed the body cavity and plugged the mouth, nose, and ears. A scarab beetle, carved in stone, was then placed over the heart. Scarabs were a symbol of life. Even the name of the scarab beetle is equivalent to the hieroglyph for "to be." Spells carved on the mummy's scarab told the dead person's heart to provide support at the moment of judgment by the gods. The torso, the hands and feet, and the arms and legs, were all bandaged separately. Finally, after the arms were crossed over the breast, the body and the limbs were wrapped up.

As much as 6,600 feet of material might go into the wrapping of a mummy, ranging from wide sheets to

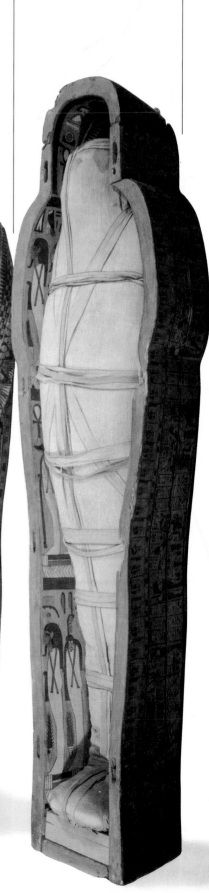

Coffin art
The inside of this coffin is richly decorated with images of the gods of the under-world. The outside is covered with useful spells in hieroglyphic writing.

BOOK OF THE DEAD

Who could resist the notion of a step-by-step guide to successful entry into the world after death? For the ancient Egyptians, the Book of the Dead provided just such a manual.

SACRED SPELLS WERE CARVED into the stone walls of the burial chamber of King Unas in his pyramid at Sāqqara, just south of present-day Cairo, about 2350 B.C. More than 200 incantations appear, the hieroglyphs picked out in pale blue-green. Known as the Pyramid Texts, they record rituals to provide the dead king with food and drink, prayers to the gods on his behalf, and magical formulas to guide him on his journey to the other world.

Pyramid Texts

Other kings of the Old Kingdom, following on from Unas, had Pyramid Texts inscribed in their pyramids, too. About 700 such spells have been deciphered.

Later on, during the Middle Kingdom, which lasted from 2050 to 1800 B.C., these magical sequences of spells were painted on the wooden coffins then used, and commoners as well as kings adopted them. Later still, during the New Kingdom, from 1550 to 1050 B.C., the spells were written out on papyrus to be entombed with the mummy. One particularly extensive version, with 165 chapters, spread across a papyrus roll 66 feet long. Modern-day archeologists who discovered these scrolls named them the *Book of the Dead*.

The *Book of the Dead* covered every worry the dead (or those about to die) might experience. A person's name was important, so one spell ensured that the dead person's spirit would remember its name. The spirit must face the judgment of the gods, so the *Book of the Dead* suggested responses for the spirit to give that made a favorable verdict certain. A wide range of spells offered protection for the dangerous journey to the other world. And there were spells to allow the spirit to revisit its earthly haunts.

The final judgment took place before the god of the underworld, Osiris. The dead person's heart, which had been left in the mummified body, was weighed against a single feather, the symbol of justice and truth. Again, the *Book of the Dead* told the spirit what to say: "My heart from my mother, do not rise against me. Do not bear witness against me. Let shouts of joy be heard when my words are weighed."

Weighing the heart
The jackal-headed god Anubis performed the weighing ceremony. A grotesque creature crouched nearby to devour the heart if it was too heavy with sin. The verdict was then recorded by the ibis-headed god Thoth, scribe to the gods.

Anubis, jackal-headed god of mummification

Thoth, ibis-headed god of wisdom, with scribe's palette

Horus, falcon-headed sky god

Osiris, god of the underworld

Dead man

Devourer of the dead

thin bandages about four inches wide. For corpses from well-to-do families, fine linen might be specially woven. The less affluent made do with torn-up sheets. In one case the sail from a boat was used, the rigging loops still visible.

Finally, after this process the mummy was usually placed in a coffin, perhaps itself modeled and painted to look like a mummy and bearing the face of the person within.

In some cases, the internal organs were preserved, too. On the principle that the dead body would require all its constituent parts for life in the here-after, the internal organs were stored in jars that accompanied the mummy through the ceremonies of mourning and interment in its final resting place, a tomb, or "house of eternity."

Ritual kit
This kit contains some of the instruments needed for the ceremony of "opening the mouth."

not do any harm to anyone. I did not make anyone work beyond their capabilities. I did not steal any offerings to the dead. I did not fornicate. I did not overcharge nor defraud by lessening the supplies. I did not divert water running into a canal. I did not deprive the gods of their choice offerings. I am pure, pure, pure."

For the wealthy classses, the eventual placing of the mummy within its final resting place might have been a ritual accompanied by a magnificent procession. Servants carried offerings of food and wine — part of the funeral ceremonies involved the ritual of "opening the mouth" of the mummy

> On the principle that the dead body needed all its constituent parts for life in the hereafter, the internal organs were stored in jars that accompanied the mummy through the ceremonies of mourning and interment.

Uncertain future

Mourning, according to the Greek historian Herodotus, who traveled to Egypt about 450 B.C., involved agitated lamentation. Leaving life gave cause for sorrow. Despite their preparations for a pleasant existence in the hereafter, the ancient Egyptians realized that they could by no means take it for granted. As one of their poems puts it: "No one has come back from there who can set our hearts at rest."

And there was the matter of eventual judgment to worry about. It took place in the Hall of the Two Truths, before the god Osiris and under the scrutiny of 42 lesser gods. The *Book of the Dead*, a guide to the underworld buried with the corpse, advises the new spirit on trial to deny any wrongdoing, although the practical listing of examples suggests that certain crimes were, in fact, all too prevalent in ancient Egypt: "I did

Organ storage
Vital organs were removed from the body, dried out, and placed in special containers called canopic jars. Each organ had its own deity, seen here on the lids of jars that date from about 640 B.C.

ROYAL BROTHERS?

Relationships within the Egyptian royal family are very confused because of apparent links so close that today they would be banned as incestuous. Amenhotep III (who ruled from 1417 to 1379 B.C.), Akhenaton's father, certainly contrived to marry his own daughter, Sitamun.

Archeologists believe that the two pharaohs who succeeded Akhenaton, Smenkhkare and Tutankhamen (whose tomb in the Valley of the Kings yielded such fabulous treasure), may well be the children of this liaison.

From their representations and a study of their skulls, Tutankhamen and Akhenaton looked so much alike that it is easy to see them as half-brothers.

to allow the departed to eat and drink in the afterlife. Priests also performed various other rituals to revive the other senses of sight, hearing, and smell.

Signs of rank, perhaps gained in service of the pharaoh, were also displayed. The coffin itself, decked with flowers, might be carried on a sledge drawn by men or oxen. Behind came the grieving family and other relatives.

Storage and security

The mummy provided the link between the world of the living and the dead. Herodotus says that mummies were kept sometimes in people's houses, perhaps in the wooden cupboards that have been found that would take a mummy standing upright and allow it to be viewed by opening up a half-length door. According to Herodotus, people in need of money would even offer the mummy of a relation as security for a loan.

Cats, dogs, and monkeys have all been found inside intricately bandaged packages, often recognizably modeled on the animal within.

Pets, too, were also transformed into mummies. Cats, dogs, and monkeys have all been found inside intricately bandaged packages, often recognizably modeled on the animal within. Archeologists speculate that these pets were preserved to provide companionship for their owner in the afterlife. Some animals, in particular cats, were mummified in huge numbers as offerings to the gods.

God incarnate

At the other extreme, a particularly sacred bull, the Apis bull, was identified from time to time. Each Apis bull was believed to be the incarnation of the supreme god. It was worshiped in life and, upon death,

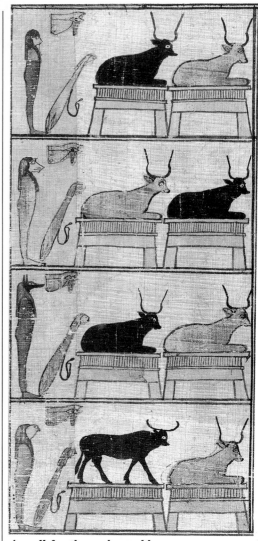

A spell for the underworld
The Seven Celestial Cows recline on shrine-shaped plinths and the Bull of Heaven stands. The Four Sons of Horus stand by the Four Rudders of Heaven, representing north, south, east, and west. This spell was to guide the deceased through the underworld.

was given a funeral. It was mummified and interred with great ceremony in a catacomb on the desert escarpment at Sâqqara. The underground galleries containing the mummies of the bulls stretch for more than 820 feet.

Examination of genetic material from identifiable royal mummies can help clarify the interrelationships between the kings that are difficult to deduce from other evidence. Data from nonroyal mummies reveal details about the life of ancient Egyptians. Disease was rife and life was often short. Most noticeably, the teeth of ancient Egyptian mummies have invariably been worn away by chewing bread made from coarse, gritty flour.

Cat mummy
This Egyptian mummified cat, stuccoed and painted, dates from about 500 B.C.

THE ENIGMA OF AKHENATON

Mighty pharaoh or henpecked husband? The character of Akhenaton has baffled Egyptologists for centuries.

Portrait of a king
Stone relief showing the odd shape of Akhenaton's head.

IMAGINE A MAN SO STRONG-MINDED that, as ruler of one of the richest countries in the ancient world, he could shift the seat of government to a new capital city, built from scratch; a man so spiritual that he introduced the worship of just one god; so artistically inclined that he patronized a new school of lively, realistic portraiture; and so family-minded that his wife and daughters figure significantly in many representations. That man was Akhenaton, king of Egypt. He probably lived about 1350 B.C., some time before the events of the biblical Exodus.

Worship of a single sun god

Akhenaton raised the worship of the Aton, the disc of the sun, above that of all the other gods of Egypt. In doing so he made a shift toward monotheism, the belief in only one god, the central concept of Judaism, Christianity, and Islam. He even changed his name from Amenhotep IV to incorporate that of the Aton. Adoration of the Aton supplanted the influence of the god Amon, whose priests had been the most powerful in the land. They regarded Akhenaton with hatred, and even removed his name from the lists of Egyptian kings.

Akhenaton founded his new capital city, Akhetaton, at a place now called Tell el Amarna, about halfway between Hermopolis (close to present-day Cairo) and Thebes, now Luxor, in the south. Paintings, freestanding sculptures, and relief carvings show scenes of worship and celebration — life in the city of Akhetaton appears to have been pleasantly luxurious.

Depictions of Akhenaton himself show a very long and thin face and a strangely shaped body, with a rounded belly and almost feminine hips. Modern-day physicians have suggested various medical conditions that might account for this odd body shape. These might have left him infertile. However, some scenes depicting his family life include several daughters.

Akhenaton's family relationships are another matter of mystery. His queen was Nefertiti. Portraits of her still in existence show an astonishing beauty. And there are hints that she was a strong personality. Some influence seems to have been at work around this period to emphasize the female side of the royal family. Many pictures of the court of Akhenaton's father, Amenhotep III, show princesses but not the princes who were also known to be present. Perhaps this increased emphasis on the female accounts for the depiction of Akhenaton's unusual body shape: Artists may have been commanded to play up feminine characteristics in their portraits of the king.

All that is known of Akhenaton's mother, Tiy, is that her father and mother were called Yuya and Thuya and were highly-placed dignitaries in the service of the king and the god Amon. Queen Tiy may well have come to Egypt from Nubia, farther to the south, making Akhenaton of partially black ancestry.

Family scene
Akhenaton and his queen, Nefertiti, are seated with their daughters. This limestone relief is from Tell el Amarna.

MUMMIES AT THE MOVIES

Why do mummies both fascinate and frighten us? Is it their facelessness or a simple horror of the walking dead? Whatever the answer, film-makers have used mummies to terrorize audiences for over 50 years.

THE CINEMA'S FASCINATION with mummified ghouls has its roots in the 1920's when the tomb of Tutankhamen was first discovered and opened by the English archeologist Howard Carter. There has long been a legend of a curse on the tomb, and the apparently strange, premature deaths of at least five of those involved with the excavation gave the legend greater weight.

It was not long before Hollywood cashed in with *The Mummy* (1932) starring Boris Karloff. The topic did not reappear until 1940, when *The Mummy's Hand* was released. This was followed rapidly by *The Mummy's Tomb* (1942), *The Mummy's Ghost*, and *The Mummy's Curse* (both 1944) — all starring Lon Chaney, Jr.

Funny mummy

The mummy was also spoofed by comics of the day in *Mummy's Dummies* (1938) with the Three Stooges, and later in *Abbott and Costello Meet the Mummy* (1955).

The mummy was allowed to rest in peace until 1959, when Britain's Hammer Studios made *The Mummy* starring Christopher Lee. The novel *The Jewel of the Seven Stars* (1904) by Bram Stoker, creator of Dracula, inspired two late entries in the mummy genre: *Blood From the Mummy's Tomb* in 1971 and *The Awakening* (1980).

The Mummy's Curse
(1944)

The Mummy (1932)
Universal Studios billed their star as "Karloff the Uncanny" for this black-and-white classic. He plays an ancient Egyptian priest buried alive for stealing a sacred scroll. He emerges 3,700 years later, and posing as a modern-day Egyptian called Ardeth Bey, he wreaks havoc in pursuit of the reincarnation of the woman he loves. He is determined to offer her the secret of eternal life, but she resists his charms.

The Mummy (1959)
In this British Hammer Studios color remake of the 1932 film, Christopher Lee plays the mummified remains of an ancient Egyptian named Kharis, who was buried alive. The mummy is found in the 19th century, brought to Britain, and then revived by an Egyptian fanatic to be his instrument of revenge. Peter Cushing plays an archeologist whose wife is the reincarnated object of Kharis's affections. This movie boasts a faster-moving mummy and is heavier on horror than the original.

The Mummy's Hand (1940)

Eight years after the first mummy movie this sequel replaced Boris Karloff with the Western star Tom Tyler donning the bandages. George Zucco plays the villainous high priest who sets the mummy Kharis on the survivors of the expedition that violated the tomb of Princess Ananka.

The Mummy's Tomb (1942)

This sequel to *The Mummy's Hand* was the first of three films in the cycle to star Lon Chaney, Jr. as the eponymous villain. George Zucco repeats his role as the evil high priest, who sends the mummy to America along with his faithful follower Turhan Bey. Their mission is to kill two survivors of an archeological expedition.

Abbott and Costello Meet the Mummy (1955)

The famous American comedy duo "met" all the great screen monsters at some time between 1948 and 1955. This Egyptian outing was the last of their horror encounters and their penultimate movie together. A missing medallion leads the heroes to a lost tomb and a living mummy called Klaris. The latter is played by Eddie Parker in an unconvincing costume.

The Awakening (1980)

Adapted from Bram Stoker's novel *The Jewel of the Seven Stars*, this glossy and blood-spattered film stars Charlton Heston as an archeologist obsessed with the tomb of an ancient Egyptian queen. As time goes by Heston begins to believe that his daughter is possessed by the spirit of the long-dead and evil queen.

EGYPTIAN MEDICINE

Detailed examination of mummies has given researchers a fascinating insight into the illnesses and injuries that were common in ancient Egypt — and the treatments used to deal with them.

IN ANCIENT EGYPT, the practice of medicine included elements of both magic and science. The pyramid architect, Imhotep, who lived about 2600 B.C., was also a priest-physician, who was later worshiped as the Egyptian god of medicine. (Imhotep was even honored by the Greeks as the equivalent of Asclepius, their god of healing.) Every area of medical specialization had its own god or goddess, and each doctor was thought to work under the influence of a particular deity. Similarly, the body was divided into 36 parts, each with its own deity; Nephthys took care of the lungs, for example, and Isis protected the liver.

Strange concoctions

Some of the remedies the Egyptians depended on — such as slivers of mouse administered for a wide range of childhood diseases, and ointments containing mud and excrement applied to infected sores — rival the disgusting concoctions of medieval witches. Others, based on sound medical principles, are still in use in some form today. Honey, for example, was used in a wide range of prescriptions, and science has confirmed that this substance not only inhibits the growth of bacteria but is also hypertonic — it draws water from cells so that they dry up.

Egyptian cure
Modern science has confirmed the efficacy of honey's medicinal properties.

Modern techniques

The Egyptians developed skilled procedures for using splints and repositioning dislocated joints, and they had sophisticated surgical techniques for dealing with broken bones. Oddly, surgery reached a peak early in ancient Egypt and then declined in popularity.

Imhotep
This priest-physician was also an astrologer and the first pyramid architect.

Healing tools
A wall relief from the temple at Kom Ombo, on the Nile north of Aswan, illustrates a range of Egyptian surgical instruments.

Historians have conjectured that later generations of Egyptians valued perfection of the body more highly, making it less permissible for doctors to cut it open. One operation that did persist was circumcision. It was performed on boys at the age of 10 by priests rather than surgeons. Another Egyptian medical practice was the adoption of a crouching position for giving birth. In modern times this has come back into favor.

Ancient complaints

Many complaints suffered by the ancient Egyptians are almost unknown in urban Western culture; few of us, for example, are troubled by crocodile bites or leprosy. Mummified remains tell us, however, that almost all Egyptians suffered an extreme form of a common modern complaint, the deterioration of their teeth. It was exacerbated by the gradual destruction of teeth by chewing unwashed food, vegetables with a high silica content,

> **Mummified remains tell us that almost all Egyptians suffered an extreme form of a modern complaint, the deterioration of their teeth.**

corn adulterated with the soft stone used for grinding it, and bread made of flour that had been inadvertently mixed with sand.

Apart from mummies, another source of knowledge about Egyptian medicine is the ancient papyri that have survived. One, discovered by the German Egyptologist Georg Ebers, is 12 inches wide and more than 68 feet long and contains more than 100 treatments. Dating from about 1500 B.C., the papyrus also records, from earlier centuries, remedies for common complaints such as headaches, diarrhea, and constipation.

Life in Egypt was harsh, and early death was common. Most of the courtiers' tombs near the Great Pyramid of Khufu at Giza belong to people who died before the age of 35.

Modern delivery
This temple relief shows a birthing stool in use.

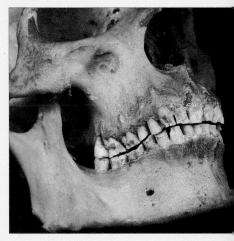

Dental decay
When he died in his early twenties, this young man had teeth that were badly worn.

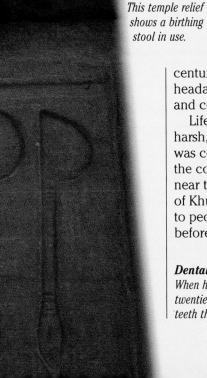

THE WONDERS OF EXODUS

The biblical story of Exodus has been interpreted in many different ways. For some it is possible that the miracles performed by Moses, the leader of the Israelites, might have some basis in fact.

IN ABOUT 1200 B.C., Merneptah, successor to Ramses II, raised up a stela, a carved stone slab, in the temple he built at Thebes, near the present-day city of Luxor. This recorded a great victory in battle. Line 27 carries hieroglyphs that spell out the name of Israel. Merneptah rejoices in his victory: "Israel is laid to waste. Its seed is no more." This inscription provides the earliest record of the name of Israel outside the Bible. However, the account of the devastation of the fledgling nation is an exaggeration. For despite the great victory recorded by Merneptah, we learn that the people of Israel had firmly established themselves in the area known as Canaan or Palestine.

The "Israel Stela"
King Merneptah recorded his victory over the Israelites on this stone slab, which was discovered in Thebes in 1896.

Leaving no trace
And that is the only reference to the people of Israel. Ancient Egypt has left no account of the events set out in the Bible in the book of Exodus. The biblical account tells how the Israelites banded together under their charismatic leader Moses, discovered their God, wandered through the wilderness and survived, and finally claimed a land of their own to the north. Nevertheless this lack of mention is understandable. Egyptian kings were used to recording victories, not defeats. In addition, a seminomadic people leave few permanent traces. And the many accidents of history ensure that any records from the distant past are likely to be patchy.

Egyptian upbringing
Moses, according to the book of Exodus, was born to the Israelites but raised by a pharaoh's daughter. The name *Moses* is Egyptian, perhaps being related to the words for "is born" or "child." Egyptian pharaohs incorporated it into their names, as, for example, did Thutmose, meaning "the child of the god Thoth" or "the

NILE DELTA

Rameses/Avaris •

Pithom •

Lake Timsa

• *Thebes*

Ancient locations
Exodus tells us that the ancestors of the people of Israel had been settled in Egypt for decades in the northeastern regions of the Nile Delta where they were forced to work on the building of the treasure cities of Pithom and Rameses. Rameses was built near the site of the earlier capital of Avaris (present-day Tell ed-Daba).

A body of water
Translations of the biblical accounts of Moses parting the waters mention the Red Sea, which lies to the south of the Gulf of Suez. It is more probable that "Red Sea" is a mistranslation of the words for "Reed Sea," which would imply a smaller, freshwater lake, crowded about with papyrus reeds, somewhere in the marshlands east of Rameses, perhaps in the region of the present-day El Qantara on the Suez Canal, or of Lake Timsah slightly to the south.

god Thoth is born." Moses fled into exile after killing an Egyptian. Then, on Mount Sinai, he encountered the burning bush.

The story is open to a number of interpretations, though none can undercut the integrity of the Bible itself. Some people, for example, speculate that Mount Sinai actually lay east of the Gulf of Aqaba, in an area of once active volcanoes. The burning bush and the descriptions of cloud, lightning, and the roaring noise that accompanied the appearance of the Lord, they also argue, might be related to volcanic phenomena. Others

---

Sacred mountain
Tradition identifies Horeb, where the miracle of the burning bush took place, with Mount Sinai, where God later appeared to Moses and the Israelites, and locates it at today's Gebel Mūsa, the mountain in the southern Sinai peninsula where the monastery of St. Catherine was later built.

MEDITERRANEAN SEA

CANAAN

SINAI PENINSULA

GULF OF AQABA

Mount Sinai/Horeb

SUEZ

RED SEA

> "And the angel of the Lord appeared to him in a flame of fire out of the midst of a bush; and he looked, and lo, the bush was burning, yet it was not consumed."
>
> **Exodus 3:2**

point out that these descriptions could apply to a desert storm, and they conjecture that the physical phenomenon of the burning bush might be explained by a bolt of lightning and the chance seepage of natural gas or petroleum.

Godly revelation
From a historical and religious perspective, however, the most important point of this incident is that God, for the first time, revealed his name to Moses and sent him back into the land of Egypt in order to persuade the pharaoh to let the people of Israel go.

The pharaoh's first reaction to Moses' demand was to increase the Israelites' work load. In return, God empowered Moses to inflict a series of plagues. Following the last plague, the death of the firstborn, the pharaoh told the Israelites to leave. Indeed, they were forced to leave in such haste that they

"Moses and the Burning Bush"
A stained-glass window by Hans Acker from the Besserer chapel in Ulm cathedral, Germany, shows Moses and the burning bush.

"Story of the Passover"
In Jewish households the story of Exodus, known as the Haggadah, is recited at the beginning of Passover. (In Hebrew the word "haggadah" means narration.) This 14th-century illuminated manuscript comes from the Golden Haggadah, which is so named because of the quantity of gold used in its design.

Mount Sinai
The harsh landscape around Mount Sinai has changed little since the time of Exodus.

could not wait for their dough to rise but had to bake unleavened bread on the road (This unleavened bread is eaten at the Jewish festival of Passover to commemorate the sparing of their firstborn in the final plague.)

At this point the people of Israel probably headed west and south toward the Sinai peninsula, rather than along the military coastal road leading to the region of Canaan. The pillar of fire that led the Israelites by night, and of cloud that led them by day, is usually explained in natural terms as coming from signal fires lit by scouts sent ahead to find the way.

The pharaoh now sent his army after the Israelites, realizing that he could not spare his work force, and trapped them against the sea. Blocked by the sea, Moses stretched out his hand, the waters divided, and the Israelites crossed — but the pursuing Egyptians were engulfed.

Freak conditions
Some interpretations suggest that freak weather conditions, such as a strong east wind, might have pushed back what may have been in reality very shallow waters to reveal drying mud or sand. The Israelites, on foot, passed over

to safety. The Egyptians, in military formation, with their horses and chariots, bogged themselves down, fell into confusion, and were trapped by the returning waters. Thus the Israelites were free to begin their seminomadic life in the wilderness, eventually making their way to the region of Canaan.

During their time in the wilderness the Israelites came to Mount Sinai, where the Lord called Moses to the mountaintop in order to instruct him regarding the Ten Commandments. When Moses returned from the mountaintop with the two stone tablets on which the commandments were written, the Israelites were terrified because he glowed so brightly. Moses "did not know that the skin of his face shone because he had been talking with God." (Exodus 34:29).

Through the ages there have been many reports of holy men surrounded by such auras. In 1973 the English scientist

> **The pharaoh sent his army after the Israelites and trapped them against the sea. Blocked by the sea, Moses stretched out his hand, the waters divided, and the Israelites crossed — but the pursuing Egyptians were engulfed.**

Dr. Lyall Watson speculated that everyone possesses an aura and that they are a physical emanation visible to people whose eyes are highly sensitive to low-frequency light. Dr. Watson suggests that an intense spirituality heightens the aura enabling others to see it.

Which pharaoh?
Exactly when the people of Israel left Egypt and which pharaoh saw plagues strike his land and people, and his army destroyed, is a matter of great conjecture.

One notion put forward is that the pharaoh involved was Ramses II, father of Merneptah (and of more than 100 other children). Ramses II built widely throughout Egypt and also reigned long enough, 60 years or more, to allow the Israelites to make their way to Canaan in time to battle against Merneptah.

Others suggest an earlier pharaoh. Messages sent to the court of Akhenaton, the Egyptian king who gave himself over to the worship of the sun disc, the Aton, and who reigned 100 years or so before Ramses II, might indicate that the people of Israel were already settled in Canaan.

Timely question

Giving accurate dates for these events is highly problematic. By most experts' calculations, the reign of the pharaoh Ramses II stretched across the middle of the 13th century B.C., putting the Exodus from Egypt at around 1250 B.C. Many scholars accept the decades around 1200 B.C. as the time when Israel established itself in the land of Canaan. Some estimates put Ramses' reign as much as 300 years later, which would make it impossible for him to be the pharaoh of the Exodus.

Yet other scholars suggest an earlier period for Exodus, about 1460 to 1420 B.C., arguing that this date ties in with the biblical statement that the Exodus from Egypt took place 480 years before the reign of Solomon. We may have some idea of what happened. But when exactly it happened is likely to remain a mystery forever.

THE PLAGUES OF EGYPT

When the pharaoh refused to allow the Israelites to leave Egypt, the Lord brought 10 terrible plagues to the land. First He instructed Moses and his brother Aaron: "Take your rod and stretch out your hand over the waters of Egypt, over their rivers, their canals, and their ponds, and all their pools of water, that they may become blood; and there shall be blood throughout all the land of Egypt, both in vessels of wood and vessels of stone." (Exodus 7:19). However, when Moses and Aaron carried out the Lord's instructions and the Nile turned red, the pharaoh still refused to let the Israelites go.

Frogs, flies, and locusts

Exodus (7:20–12:29) lists the plagues that followed: frogs proliferated, then died; lice attacked people and animals; swarms of flies appeared; Egyptian cattle fell ill and died while those of the people of Israel did not; boils affected people and cattle; a massive hailstorm destroyed the crops; locusts swarmed everywhere; and darkness fell for three days. But still the pharaoh would not capitulate.

Finally, the Lord sent the last and the most devastating plague: "All the first-born in the land of Egypt shall die, from the first-born of Pharaoh who sits upon his throne, even to the first-born of the maidservant who is behind the mill; and all the first-born of the cattle. And there shall be a great cry throughout the land of Egypt,

The plagues strike
Four of the "Plagues of Egypt" (left and above) as seen in the 14th-century Jewish manuscript the Golden Haggadah.

such as there has never been, nor ever shall be again." (Exodus 11:5–6). It was only after the last plague that the pharaoh finally allowed the Israelites to leave Egypt.

Natural phenomena

Several of the plagues might be explained as natural phenomena. For the Nile does turn red with silt and locusts do swarm from time to time. Exodus says the locusts came on a wind and were carried away by another, which might sound like a typical locust swarm. It may be that even the last plague could have been caused by some epidemic. Yet its significance lies in the fact that the Israelites were spared. There is no explanation for the fact that an entire race managed to avoid such a tragic loss.

THE QUEEN OF SHEBA

The Queen of Sheba is one of the shadowy figures of ancient history. Is it possible that she and Hatshepsut, the first female pharaoh of Egypt, were one and the same?

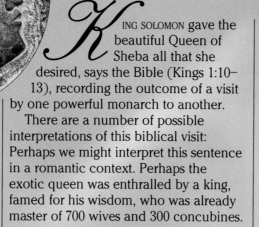

Abyssinian queen
Stone relief carving of the Queen of Sheba from Ethiopia, where she is thought to be a founder of the royal dynasty.

KING SOLOMON gave the beautiful Queen of Sheba all that she desired, says the Bible (Kings 1:10–13), recording the outcome of a visit by one powerful monarch to another.

There are a number of possible interpretations of this biblical visit: Perhaps we might interpret this sentence in a romantic context. Perhaps the exotic queen was enthralled by a king, famed for his wisdom, who was already master of 700 wives and 300 concubines.

Intellectual attraction?

Perhaps the attraction was intellectual. The Bible states that the queen came to ask questions of Solomon and that he answered every one. One riddle she is traditionally believed to have asked the wise Solomon is: "What has ten holes; when one is open, nine are closed; when the one closes, nine are open?" The answer is: a human being, whose navel closes following birth.

According to Arab tradition, the queen tested Solomon's shrewdness further by producing a mix of real and artificial flowers and challenging him to tell one from the other. Solomon had the windows opened wide — bees flew in and quickly revealed the real flowers. Then it was Solomon's turn. He bet the queen that she could not resist touching any of the beautiful objects in her guest chamber. At stake, he said, was her virtue. He then served her a magnificent meal of spicy food. During the night, the queen became thirsty and helped herself to a glass of water and so lost the wager.

Regal arrival

Perhaps the encounter was basically competitive. The queen, arriving with her show of riches and her list of questions, hoped to discomfit the fabled king.

Solomon, however, had riches of his own. His domain stretched from the River Euphrates to the border of Egypt. He was also, according to tradition, the source of wisdom, the author of 3,000 proverbs, including among them his own vindication: "It is the glory of God to conceal; the honour of kings to search out."

A simpler interpretation of their fabled meeting is that it may have centered around negotiations over trade routes. The Queen of Sheba, impressed by King Solomon's power, offered him the gold, spices, and precious stones detailed in the Bible in return for trade concessions.

Trade negotiations

Diplomatic niceties presumably explain her compliments to the king on his wisdom and life-style. The reality was that Solomon had initiated shipping ventures along the length of the Red Sea that would undercut the livelihood of those dependent on camel caravans. It seems that the king and queen may have struck some sort of bargain over who would trade where.

This theory places the Queen of Sheba as traveling from somewhere south of Palestine, but exactly where is still a mystery. Quite possibly she came from southern Arabia, in the area that is now Yemen. This was certainly a region that was central

Royal visit
Artistic reconstruction (in 17th-century dress) of the meeting of the Queen of Sheba and King Solomon, by Frans Francken the Elder (1542–1616).

to the caravan routes that depended on camels to transport spices and the like over much of Arabia.

Possibly she might have come from Ethiopia. Here, too, trade was important and Egyptian domination of the area was breaking down. Ethiopian chronicles purportedly trace the foundation of the kingdom back to Menelik, who is said to be the son of the Queen of Sheba and

> The queen tested Solomon's shrewdness by producing a mix of real and artificial flowers and challenging him to tell one from the other. Solomon had the windows opened wide — bees flew in and quickly revealed the real flowers.

Solomon. Paintings showing the meeting suggest that the queen included lions among her gifts to the king, which would also support an Ethiopian origin.

Female pharaoh
The identity of the Queen of Sheba has also been linked with Hatshepsut, the woman who became the first female pharaoh of Egypt. Hatshepsut is remembered for the temple she built on the west bank of the Nile across the river from Thebes; for inscriptions she had carved extolling her beauty; and for making a trading expedition to the "Land of Punt."

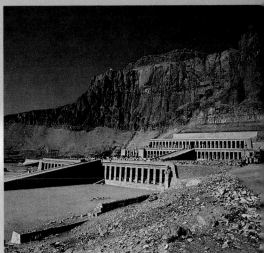

Royal burial temple
The funerary temple of Queen Hatshepsut lay on the west bank of the Nile at Dayr al-Bahri, across the river from the ancient city of Thebes.

Most authorities locate Punt somewhere along the Red Sea, perhaps as far as present-day Somalia or even on the other side, on the coast of Arabia.

Continuing mystery
However, this link would require some very heavy recasting of chronological dates. Solomon's reign, of 40 years, is customarily placed about 950 B.C. And Hatshepsut lived, by most accepted calculations, several hundred years earlier than this.

Arab history and legend differ from the Bible in some respects. Even though the Bible does not actually give the name of the Queen of Sheba, in the Koran she is known as Balkis or Bilkis.

Arab sources reveal that her kingdom was Saba, an area in southwest Arabia (now Yemen) that had become rich from trade, and her capital city was Mariaba, the present-day Ma'rib. There archeologists have found the ruins of a great palace. Perhaps this city was the real home of the mysterious Queen of Sheba.

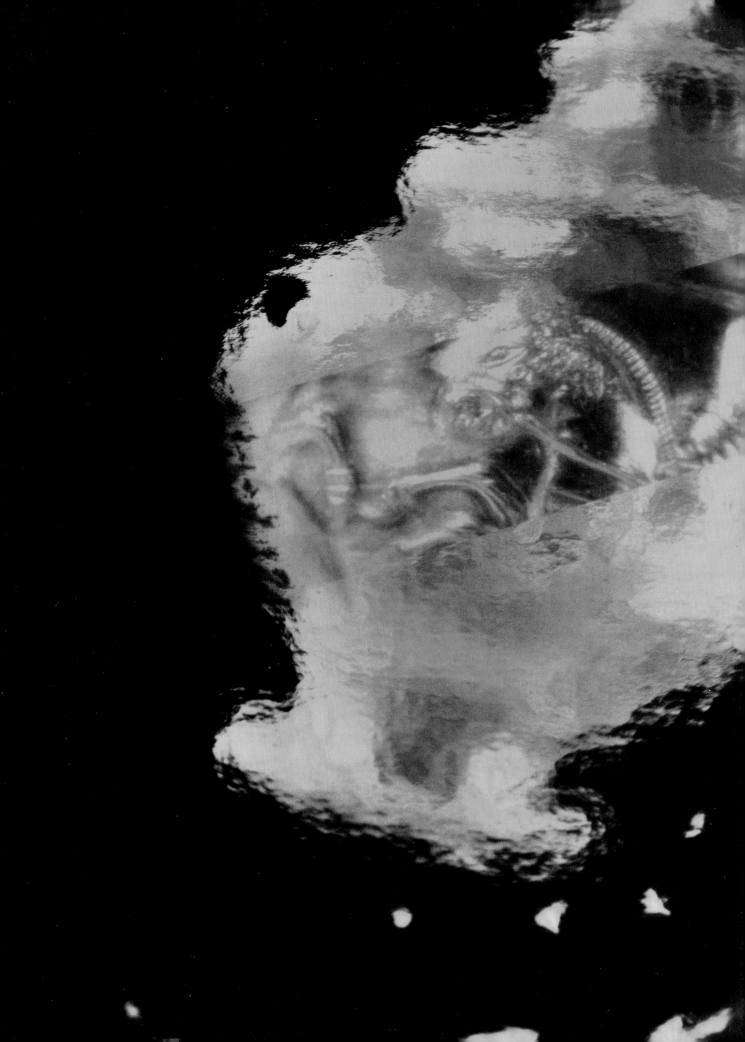

CHAPTER FOUR

MYSTERIOUS RELICS

Giant statues, ritual buildings, ornate gold artifacts arranged in complex burial grounds, and an underground army of terra-cotta soldiers — each new archeological discovery challenges the assumptions of the experts on ancient civilizations.

In ancient times the Thracians inhabited the region that forms present-day northern Greece, Bulgaria, and southern Romania. They never developed a written language but the Thracians left behind a rich legacy of skillfully designed artifacts: ornaments, jewelry, vessels, and armor.

The ancient Greeks admired the Thracian warriors for their horsemanship, chariots, and the splendor of their armor. In Homer's epic poem the *Iliad*, written in the eighth century B.C., the Thracian king Rhesos, who took part in the siege of the city of Troy,

God at work
In Greek mythology, Hephaestus was the god of metalworking. He is depicted at work at his forge on this Greek vase, which dates from about 500 B.C.

MAGICAL METALWORKERS

In ancient times, smiths were frequently regarded as magicians. Historians believe that smiths may have held a position of great social and religious significance in Thracian society.

Among the Phrygians, a Thracian people who migrated to Asia Minor in the second millennium B.C., smiths were associated with the Great Goddess, the universal mother, who symbolized fertility and whose influence extended over plants, animals, and humans.

In Greek mythology, the Cabeiri were the sons of Hephaestus, the god of metalworking. They were known as the smith-deities, and the cult associated with them, which appears to have been of Phrygian, or Thracian, origin, survived into classical times.

is described as a splendid figure. "His are the finest horses I have seen and the largest — whiter than snow, and like the winds when they run. His chariot is a beautiful work of gold and silver. And he has come with prodigious armour made of gold — such things should not be worn by mortal men, but rather by the immortal gods."

Archeological discoveries in the 20th century have shown that the Thracians were skilled metalworkers. Copper appears to have been used first for metalworking in Thrace between 5000 and 3000 B.C. Known as the Chalcolithic period, this epoch occurred at the end of the Neolithic Age and before the beginning of the Bronze Age.

A number of copper mines have been found in Bulgaria that appear to date

from about 4200 B.C. One mine, located near the city of Stara Zagora, in central Bulgaria, has pits up to 400 yards long, with shafts 60 feet deep, indicating that mining was carried out on a large scale. Artifacts from this period include ornaments, beads, and trinkets as well as tools and weapons.

Archeologists had believed that metalworking first began in the Middle East, and that these techniques spread to other parts of the world, possibly being carried by traveling smiths. However, the discovery of such mines as Stara Zagora suggest that metalworking began independently in a number of different places, including Thrace.

Forging of a people

The story of who the Thracians were and where they originated stretches back to prehistoric times. Archeologists believe that the Thracians were made up of many different tribes, spread across a vast geographical area. The earliest

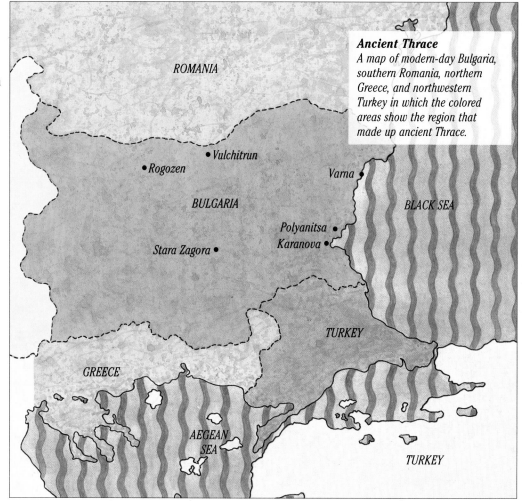

Ancient Thrace
A map of modern-day Bulgaria, southern Romania, northern Greece, and northwestern Turkey in which the colored areas show the region that made up ancient Thrace.

ROMANIA

• Vulchitrun

• Rogozen

Varna •

BULGARIA

BLACK SEA

Polyanitsa •
Karanova •

Stara Zagora •

TURKEY

GREECE

AEGEAN
SEA

TURKEY

settlers in the region that came to be known as Thrace appear to have been Neolithic farmers from Asia, who arrived in the seventh millennium B.C., having been drawn to the fertile lowlands of southeast Europe. In the millennia that followed, numerous other tribes arrived in the region, usually coming round the northern shores of the Black Sea from central Asia.

Incised pottery

Archeological evidence suggests that during the Chalcolithic period a prosperous and surprisingly advanced society developed in Thrace. A settlement at Polyanitsa (now in southeastern Bulgaria), for example, founded in the early part of the Chalcolithic era, appears to have been constructed according to a sophisticated plan. Incised pottery also suggests that a rudimentary form of writing existed. A 5,500-year-old clay plaque, for example, was found at Karanovo in Bulgaria. Some experts believe it is writing; others argue that the markings may simply represent religious symbols.

Destructive migrators

At the end of the Chalcolithic era, about 3000 B.C., a new wave of migration from the north by a people known as the Yamnaya culture wiped out all the progress that had been made. Existing villages were destroyed and their culture lost.

Destructive as they may have been, the invading Yamnaya people introduced two vitally important developments into Thracian culture: the wheeled cart and the domesticated horse. Thereafter the Thracians became highly regarded as great horsemen and horsebreeders.

Historians have even suggested that Thracian horsemen were the source for the mythical creatures, part man, part horse, known as centaurs. The reason: Greek footsoldiers may have originated this myth by simply misidentifying marauding Thracian horsemen as single creatures.

Thracian spoon
A three-headed golden spoon was found at Vulchitrun, northern Bulgaria. Archeologists believe that it may have been used in some religious ritual.

Revival of skills

Metalworking seems to have declined in Thrace during the early part of the Bronze Age, only to revive about 2500 B.C.

During the 20th century caches of breathtaking treasure have been unearthed throughout Bulgaria. In 1920 at Vulchitrun, in northern Bulgaria, a farmer's spade turned up 13 solid gold objects, which weighed more than 27 pounds. These included elegantly designed cups, vessels with lids, and a curious triple spoon. The find dates from about 1100 B.C. and is believed to have formed part of some collection of ritual objects that may have been hidden at a time of crisis.

A farmer's spade turned up 13 solid gold objects, which weighed more than 27 pounds. These included elegantly designed cups, vessels with lids, and a curious triple spoon.

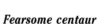
Fearsome centaur
A centaur, a mythical creature that was part man, part horse, tramples down an enemy. This relief sculpture formed part of the decoration on the Parthenon temple on the Acropolis in Athens, which was built in the fifth century B.C.

Followers of Dionysus
This Roman terra-cotta relief from the first century A.D. shows a Maenad and a male follower of Dionysus. The dancing pair are depicted holding the infant god in a cradle between them.

DIONYSIAN REVELERS
In ancient Greece and Rome the god Dionysus (called Bacchus by the Romans) was the god of fruitfulness and especially wine. The association with wine led to Dionysus being linked with drunkenness, debauchery, and disorder. Revels led by the god were called *orgi* (meaning "rites"), from which the English word orgy is derived.

The followers of Dionysus were traditionally women, who were known as Maenads. The god was said to cause such frenzy that these women abandoned their homes to follow where the god led. Wearing animal skins, and wreathed with ivy, the Maenads were notorious for their wild dancing, lewdness, and savagery.

Thracian huntress
This silver gilt jug from the Rogozen treasure shows the Thracian goddess Bendis, holding a bow and arrow, riding on a lioness. The goddess, like her ancient Greek counterpart Artemis, was associated with hunting and warfare.

More recently, in 1985, in the tiny village of Rogozen, in the Vratsa district of northwestern Bulgaria, a hoard of 165 silver vessels, some of which were gilded, was unearthed from an empty plot that had once been used as a vegetable garden. The discovery of the treasure, which dates from the fourth century B.C., has caused archeologists to reexamine their belief that traveling metalworkers were responsible for the work. Inscriptions found on various vessels indicate that metal workshops were established in several locations throughout Thrace.

Warrior aristocracy
Archeologists believe that by the fifth century B.C. Thracian tribes were ruled by chiefs and organized into a warrior aristocracy in which women did the majority of the work while men concentrated on fighting and horse breeding. These Thracian chieftains

seem to have maintained their authority by establishing traveling courts, moving between fortified residences. Each of these headquarters appears to have had its own workshop where the gold, which was collected as both taxes and gifts, was transformed into objects.

Revealing treasure
The Rogozen treasure represents the flowering of Thracian culture, and gives an insight into Thracian religious beliefs. They seem to have centered round a Great Goddess and her son-and-lover, a dying god who represented the life cycle of vegetation.

This son may be connected with the unnamed Thracian hero figure who appears repeatedly in archeological finds. He is nearly always shown riding a horse, either hunting or returning to the welcome of a female figure. It appears that by overcoming evil the hero might then return to the Great Goddess and attain immortality, which the Thracians believed awaited them in the afterlife.

The Greek historian Herodotus, writing in the fifth century B.C., remarked that the Thracians worshiped only Ares, Dionysus, and Artemis. This view may reflect the Greeks' belief that the Thracians' main preoccupations were the fighting, drinking, and hunting that these deities represent. The Greeks also believed that Dionysus, the god of wine and ecstasy, was originally a Thracian god. Followers of this deity were believed to indulge in the drunkenness and debauchery that Dionysus represented.

Another mythological figure believed to have come from Thrace was Orpheus. A skilled musician, he represented the opposite of Dionysian practices, such as celibacy and abstinence from alcohol. In myth, Orpheus met his death by being torn limb from limb by Dionysus' savage female followers, the Maenads.

Apart from the few hints gleaned from classical mythology, the Thracians remain a mysterious race. In the absence of a written record, only their fabulous treasure can give us any clues to the secrets of their rich culture.

GRAVES OF GOLD

Bracelets, beads, diadems, and rings — wonderful jewelry hammered out of gold. The artistry and skill of the ancient people who crafted these exquisite artifacts continue to astound archeologists.

Golden features
Some of the graves held life-size clay masks of heads with features represented in gold.

I

N THE FALL OF 1972, at Varna, on the Black Sea coast of modern Bulgaria, a tractor operator named Raicho Marinov was excavating a five-foot trench for an electric cable when he noticed pieces of shiny yellow sheet metal. Marinov had unearthed an ancient burial ground, which was found to date from around 3000 B.C. Along with flint knives and stone tools and a number of copper axes, investigators found a quantity of finely crafted gold jewelry.

More than 30 of the graves have been uncovered so far. Yet none contains a body; they appear to have been symbolic burial places. In some of these empty graves, the dead person was represented by a clay mask placed where the head might normally lie, a mask often decorated with gold jewelry.

Golden decoration

The golden grave goods came in various shapes and sizes. There was a great number of gold plaques, about an inch across, with holes bored in them so that they could be sewn onto clothing. Many were simple geometric shapes, but there were also a large number of plaques representing horned animals, which appear to have been of great importance to the local inhabitants. Gold beads were also enormously popular, and one tomb contained no fewer than eight strings of them, the longest containing 257 beads. Other finds included rings, bracelets, diadems, golden spirals, and models of knucklebones.

The wealth of chiefs

Also among the finds were a number of golden scepters and ceremonial weapons, which suggests that some of the graves were those of chiefs or rulers. Other graves were uncovered which were less rich in gold artifacts.

The wearing of gold
The Varna artifacts may have been used for decoration. The animals (top) and the beaten plaque (bottom) are pierced with holes by which they could be attached to clothing.

This difference has led archeologists to suggest that Varna society may have been organized so that a wealthy aristocracy ruled over the poorer villagers.

Most of the golden objects appear to have been beaten into shape rather than forged, suggesting that metallurgical techniques were still fairly primitive at the time. The fact that at Varna gold objects far out-

> **There was a great number of gold plaques, with holes bored in them so that they could be sewn onto clothing.**

number copper ones has led investigators, such as the British archeologist Prof. Colin Renfrew of Cambridge University, to suggest that metalworking first began not because metal implements were useful, but to make objects of conspicuous display. In the ancient world the Thracians were noted for the gold ornaments they wore. The exquisite artifacts found at Varna give us an indication just how splendid the Thracians must have looked when they were decked out in all their finery.

A tower to touch heaven
The biblical account of the building of the Tower of Babel has inspired many artists. This richly detailed painting of the building of the tower is by the Flemish master Pieter Brueghel the Elder (c.1525–69).

THE LEGENDARY TOWER OF BABEL

Could the remains of a great tower, found on the site of the ancient city of Babylon, be the same tower that is described in the Bible?

*I*N 587 B.C. THE CITY OF JERUSALEM was destroyed by the Babylonian king Nebuchadnezzar. The Jews were taken into exile to the mighty city of Babylon, situated on the fertile banks of the River Euphrates, near the modern town of Al Hilla, south of Baghdad, in present-day Iraq. The Jews remained in exile in Babylon between 586 and 538 B.C. During that time, scholars have established that much of the Bible was written in its present form.

The account of the building of the Tower of Babel appears in the Old Testament in the middle of a long genealogical list of the descendants of Noah:

Now the whole earth had one language and few words. And as men migrated from the east, they found a plain in the land of Shinar and settled there. And they said to one another, "Come, let us make bricks, and burn them thoroughly." And they had brick for stone, and bitumen for mortar. Then they said, "Come, let us build ourselves a city, and a tower with its top in the heavens, and let us make a name for ourselves" (Genesis 11:1–4).

The passage goes on to relate how God came down from heaven to see the tower, and how He threw the languages of humankind into confusion so as to prevent its completion. And because this was the place of confusion of tongues, or "babble," it was called Babel.

A vast and fertile plain

The "land of Shinar" is known to refer to the land of Mesopotamia, lying between the Tigris and Euphrates rivers, which forms present-day Iraq. This vast and fertile plain was first settled by farming communities as early as the sixth millennium B.C., and cities appeared in the fourth millennium B.C. The original city builders were the Sumerians, but over the centuries a number of immigrants and invaders occupied the land, including the Akkadians, Assyrians, and Chaldeans.

Mighty ziggurat
The remains of great towers, called ziggurats, are found on the sites of many ancient Babylonian cities. These remains are from near the town of Shush in Iran.

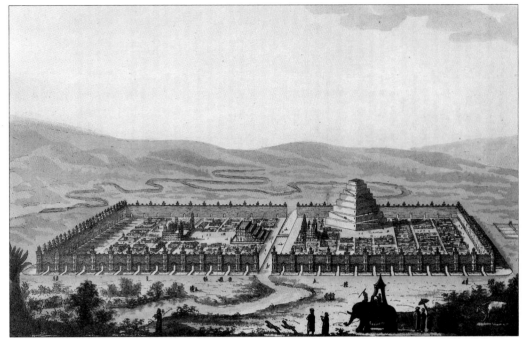

Walled city
This 19th-century Italian engraving shows an interpretation of what the city of Babylon might have looked like, based on eyewitness accounts left by visitors to the ancient city.

ANCIENT EYEWITNESS

The Greek historian Herodotus traveled widely throughout the ancient world. In the fifth century B.C. he visited Babylon, and his account provides an intriguing record of the city at the time of its greatness.

"It [Babylon] lies in a great plain, and is in shape a square, each side an hundred furlongs in length; thus four hundred and eighty furlongs make the complete circuit of the city. Such is the size of the city of Babylon; and it was planned like no other city whereof we know."

Herodotus also described the great ziggurat, a huge tower, which was one of the most eye-catching sights in the city:

"In the midmost of one division of the city stands the royal palace, surrounded by a high and strong wall....In the center of this enclosure a solid tower has been built, of one furlong's length and breadth; a second tower rises from this, and from it yet another, till at last there are eight. The way up to them mounts spirally outside all the towers; about halfway in the ascent is a halting place, with seats for repose, where those who ascend sit down and rest."

Babylonian god
Marduk was the supreme god of the Babylonians. He is represented here in the form of a lion. This terra-cotta figure dates from the sixth century B.C.

The Jews' ancestors were said to have come from the land of Shinar, and the prophet Abraham (who lived early in the second millennium B.C.) was from the Sumerian city of Ur in southern Iraq.

The Mesopotamian plains were almost entirely lacking in stone. From the beginning of the Sumerian civilization any kind of construction was carried out using mud bricks, which had been either fired or sun dried. These were often cemented together with bitumen, which occurs naturally in the area.

City of bricks

By far the largest and most impressive of these mud-brick cities was Babylon. It was said to be the site of the legendary Hanging Gardens, one of the Seven Wonders of the Ancient World. The name of the city is first found in the Akkadian language, as *Bab-ilim*. It is believed to have developed from an earlier word, *Babil*, the meaning of which is uncertain. Later the city was known as *Bab-ilani*, meaning "gate of the gods." From this comes the name Babylon. From Babil to Babel is only a short step in pronunciation. The name of the city appears to have been misinterpreted by the Jewish exiles as being related to the Hebrew word *balal*, meaning "confusion."

At the time of the Jewish exile in Babylon, the city was already established as a cosmopolitan trading center. Some historians have suggested that Jewish travelers, finding themselves among a

Astonishing buildings, called ziggurats, which soared above all other surrounding buildings, were to be found in almost every city throughout Mesopotamia.

large number of foreigners speaking different languages, may have assumed that the ensuing linguistic confusion gave the city its name.

Archeological remains, however, have established that in Mesopotamia towers were actually constructed in the form described in the account of the Tower of Babel in the Bible. From Sumerian times onward these astonishing buildings, called ziggurats, which soared above all other surrounding buildings, were to be found in almost every city throughout the land of Mesopotamia.

The word ziggurat is, in fact, of Assyro-Babylonian origin, and means a pinnacle or mountaintop. Built of solid mud brick, the ziggurat had a square, or oblong, base and usually consisted of several stories, most commonly three, five, or seven. Each story was smaller than the one below and of the same geometric shape as the base, rising in a series of steps, or tiers, and having a small temple placed on the uppermost pinnacle.

Patron deities

Archeologists believe that the Sumerians first began to build ziggurats near the end of the fourth millennium B.C. Normally part of a complex of religious buildings, a ziggurat would be situated in a large open courtyard, which was surrounded by other temples. The ziggurat temple was usually dedicated to the patron deity of the city: to Marduk at Babylon, to the moon god Nannar at Ur in southern Iraq. Other deities had their temples elsewhere within the city walls.

By far the most impressive of these buildings was the great ziggurat at Babylon. The first tower, attributed to King Hammurabi (1792–1750 B.C.), seems to have been largely destroyed by the time the Assyrian king Sennacherib conquered the city in 689 B.C. it was later rebuilt by the Chaldean kings Nabopolassar (625–605 B.C.) and his son Nebuchadnezzar (604–562 B.C.), under whom Babylon reached its greatest glory.

Visible for miles

The great ziggurat at Babylon was about 290 feet tall, built of 58 million bricks, and was visible for a distance of more than 60 miles. Its name was *Etemenanki*, which has been variously translated as "The Foundation Stone of Heaven and Earth" or "The House of the Foundation Stone of Heaven and Earth."

Babylonian splendor
An early 20th-century German magazine illustration visualizes the temple of Marduk in Babylon. Public interest in Babylon increased following the excavation of the site of the city between 1899 and 1917.

An inscription written at the command of Nabopolassar has been found on the site of Babylon, and it refers to Etemenanki. It records that the god Marduk, the supreme deity in the Babylonian pantheon, commanded Nabopolassar to repair the ziggurat and to "make its foundations secure in the bosom of the nether world and make its summit like the heavens." Another inscription, this time by the ruler Nebuchadnezzar, says: "To raise up the top of Etemenanki that it might rival heaven, I laid to my hand."

Jewish exiles, who had themselves been brought to the city of Babylon during Nebuchadnezzar's reign, may well have been familiar with these inscriptions. Together with the name Etemenanki, itself linking earth and heaven, it is easy to see how the inscriptions gave rise to the idea of men building "a tower, with its top in the heavens."

Heavenly aspirations

It would have certainly been apparent to the Jewish exiles that the great ziggurat of Nebuchadnezzar was not the original but rather a rebuilding or repair. The first tower, constructed with the same aspirations toward heaven, had been overthrown at some earlier time, either by King Sennacherib, or perhaps, if one wished to interpret it in this way, by the very hand of God himself.

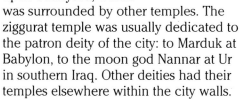

Receiving the law
King Hammurabi, builder of the first "Tower of Babel" receives the code of law from Shamash, the god of justice. This carved stone tablet dates from about 1700 B.C.

THE SECRETS OF THE EXTERNSTEINE

The bizarre rock formation known as the Externsteine is a link with Germany's pagan Saxon past. A lack of evidence about the ceremonies performed there has led historians to some wild speculations.

THE DRAMATIC NATURAL ROCK FORMATION known as the Externsteine in the Teutoburger Wald near Detmold in northwest Germany, was the goal of pilgrims in prehistoric, Celtic, and Saxon times. It has been suggested that the stones, like the stone circles of Britain and Ireland, were used to work out solar alignments in ancient times. The main axis of doorways and entrances in the Externsteine is toward the northeast, the direction of sunrise at midsummer. The rooms that appear to be cut out of rock are believed to have been observation chambers or places where occult rituals were performed.

Prehistorians have established that the rites and ceremonies of the pagan Saxons included worship at stones, which were seen as places of spirit. There are many other ancient rock sanctuaries in Germany, but none is as spectacular as the Externsteine.

Christian champion
Charlemagne (A.D. 742–814), Holy Roman Emperor and king of the Franks, conquered most of continental Europe and suppressed paganism.

Destruction of shrines

In the year A.D. 772, after a war lasting more than 30 years, the Holy Roman Emperor Charlemagne destroyed the shrines of Saxon paganism in mainland Europe. Worship at sacred stones, including the Externsteine, was prohibited. It was then that the ancient pagan rituals ceased or were driven underground, to be practiced in secret. The written history of the Externsteine begins in 1093, when it was owned by the bishop of Paderborn, a town about 15 miles to the south. Cistercian monks from Paderborn are said to have worshiped at the Externsteine, and even lived there. When the monastery at Paderborn was finally abandoned, the Externsteine ceased to have any religious connections. A local landowner used it variously as a stone quarry and a hunting lodge. Then, in the 17th century, the rocks were used as a military fortress.

Early in the 20th century, nationalistic German prehistorians began to make exaggerated claims that ancient Germans were superior in every way to their

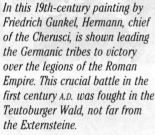

A decisive battle
In this 19th-century painting by Friedrich Gunkel, Hermann, chief of the Cherusci, is shown leading the Germanic tribes to victory over the legions of the Roman Empire. This crucial battle in the first century A.D. was fought in the Teutoburger Wald, not far from the Externsteine.

neighbors. The leading figure in this movement was Wilhelm Teudt, whose influential book, *Germanische Heiligtümer (Ancient German Sanctuaries)*, was published in 1929. Heinrich Himmler, chief of Hitler's S.S., was interested in esoteric subjects. When the Nazis seized power, Himmler became Teudt's patron.

Useful propaganda

The Externsteine had associations that proved very useful to Nazi propagandists. Close by was the site of the battle in the Teutoburger Wald where, in the year A.D. 9, Germanic armies under Hermann, chief of the Cherusci tribe, had defeated the mighty legions of Rome. This battle prevented the Germanic tribes from coming under the yoke of the Roman Empire.

Wilhelm Teudt (1860–1942)

> ## The Nazis intended that the Externsteine would show the world the historical superiority of the ancient German peoples over their neighbors.

Once Teudt had Nazi patronage, academics no longer dared criticize his theories, which became state orthodoxy. Himmler appointed Teudt director of an ambitious project to "restore" the Externsteine. The Nazis intended that the site would show the rest of the world the historical superiority of the ancient German peoples over their neighbors. Exhibitions of German antiquities, heralded by Nazi ceremonies, would further reinforce the propaganda message. Excavations began on the site, but the Second World War put a stop to the project.

The Externsteine in the New Age

After the war, the Externsteine was named a national heritage site, and a lake was constructed to enhance its picturesque qualities. But the officials who made it a "nature monument" could not have foreseen its resurgence as a sacred place. Today, it is the haunt of many esoteric groups, ranging from witches to New Age followers of native American religions and even latter-day followers of Wilhelm Teudt.

Medieval carving
About A.D. 1120, Cistercian monks carved a relief at the site. It shows the body of Jesus being taken down from the cross. Nicodemus stands on a stool formed from the bent pagan world pillar, Irminsul. This symbolizes the victory of Christianity over paganism.

Sacred heartland of Saxony
The countryside around the Externsteine is rich in mysterious landscape features, such as standing stones, carved stones, hermit caves, and alleged ley lines. The Externsteine rocks themselves have been much modified by man over the centuries. There are platforms, steps, slots, niches, viewing apertures, and chambers, including what is believed to be a chapel at the top of the most prominent pillar.

SONS OF TROY?

Preserved in the epic poems of Homer, the tale of the war between the Greeks and Trojans is one of the most powerful legends of Western civilization. Yet until an astonishing 19th-century archeological find, the existence of Troy was thought to be little more than an intriguing myth.

IN 1870, FOLLOWING UP CLUES found in Homer's *Iliad*, the German archeologist Heinrich Schliemann began looking for the city of Troy in the area around Hisarlik on the coast of northwestern Turkey. By 1873 Schliemann had found the site of an ancient city. And suddenly it became possible to consider that the city of Troy had actually existed.

Further excavation has revealed that at least nine cities existed on the site of Hisarlik, from the Bronze Age (about 3000 B.C.) until Roman times. One of them, which archeologists call Troy VII A, was destroyed at approximately the same period as the traditional date

> To the ancient Greeks, Homer's *Iliad* and *Odyssey* were both true records and great literature. It was on this tide of literature and belief that the legend of Troy was swept forward into later centuries.

of the Trojan War, in the 12th century B.C. But whether the war as described by Homer ever took place remains in dispute. Some circumstantial evidence does suggest that Homer, writing four centuries later, was referring to historical events. Yet we cannot prove the reality of heroes such as Achilles, Hector, and Odysseus.

The wanderings of Aeneas

To the ancient Greeks, Homer's *Iliad* and *Odyssey* were both true records and great literature. It was on this tide of literature and belief that the compelling legend of Troy was swept forward into later centuries. While literary tradition records a number of Trojan survivors of the war, by far the most important was Aeneas. He is said to have led his family and companions to Italy, where he founded the city of Lavinium in the territory that was to become Rome. Thirty years later his son, Ascanius, founded the city of Alba Longa. From this line of Alban kings came Romulus and Remus, the legendary twins who founded Rome in about 750 B.C.

THE TROJAN WAR

According to Greek legend, Paris, the youngest son of Priam, the king of Troy, was chosen by Zeus to judge which of three goddesses was the most beautiful.

The judgment of Paris

Each of the goddesses offered Paris a bribe in an effort to win the contest: Hera offered him kingly power; Athena, military might; and Aphrodite, the love of Helen of Sparta, the most beautiful woman in all the world. Paris did not hesitate in choosing Aphrodite's prize, and with the goddess's help he seduced Helen and fled with her to Troy.

Helen, however, was already married to Menelaus, king of Sparta. Paris refused to return Helen to her husband, which caused the Trojan War.

The besieged city

A thousand Greek ships set sail intent on destroying Troy. For 10 long years the Greek invaders, including the famous warriors Agamemnon, Achilles, and Odysseus, remained encamped outside the city. During this time many combats took place beneath the city walls. But the Greeks still came no closer to sacking the city.

The Trojan horse

Then one morning the Trojans saw to their astonishment that the invaders had gone. Outside the city walls stood a gigantic wooden horse. After much discussion, the Trojans wheeled the horse inside the city walls and made ready to celebrate their liberation from the Greeks.

That night the inhabitants of Troy, overjoyed that at last the long siege was over, held a great feast. But while the city slept, a secret trapdoor in the belly of the horse slid back and 50 of the most daring of the Greek warriors climbed down from the horse. Meeting with no resistance, they ransacked the city, slaughtering all who stood in their way. By dawn many of the Trojan warriors were slain, and their wives and children were carried off into slavery.

The escape of Aeneas from Troy is first mentioned by the Sicilian historian Timaeus in the fourth century B.C., but it gained its fullest form with the Roman poet Virgil (70–19 B.C.), whose great epic poem, the *Aeneid*, held the same

"The Departure of Aeneas"
An oil painting by the Italian artist Giuseppe Marchese (1699–1771) shows an idealized representation of Aeneas' departure from the city of Troy.

position in the Latin-speaking world as the Homeric poems had for the Greeks.

By the time Rome became a political power in the ancient world, its culture had been swamped by Greek influences, coming both from the Greek colonies in southern Italy and from the Etruscans, who had imported both goods and culture from Greece. The Etruscans were the dominant power in Italy when Rome was founded and were themselves believed to have emigrated from the land of Lydia, not far from Troy. Whatever the Etruscans' origin, Aeneas was a popular figure in their tradition.

By Virgil's time the Romans had already conquered the Mediterranean world, but they perhaps still felt culturally inferior to the ancient Greeks. The legend of Aeneas enabled the Romans to claim that they were descended from the "Sons of Troy." This also provided a legendary and cultural history for Rome that established it in the mainstream of classical development.

Heroic survivor

For the Romans the noble Aeneas, after superhuman struggles, succeeded in founding a yet more glorious state than his original home. At the time Virgil was writing, Aeneas' descendants had "avenged" themselves on the Greek ravagers of Troy and could be seen as having reestablished the ancient Trojan virtues. Virgil himself was probably of Etruscan stock, so the Aeneas legend may have been a favorite of his.

In early medieval Europe, when Latin was the language of scholars, the *Aeneid* remained better known than the Homeric poems. It was Virgil's epic poem more than anything else that carried forward the tale of the Sons of Troy into the mainstream of European culture.

But the tale of Trojan colonization did not end in Italy. Ancient British legend claimed that the island of

Heroic struggle
This fifth-century B.C. plate from Rhodes depicts the scene in the Iliad *in which Menelaus, having killed the Trojan Euphorbus, is attacked by Hector, the brother of Paris.*

Britain derived its name from Brutus, a Trojan. Brutus, so the story goes, was the great-grandson of Aeneas. He had been banished from Italy after accidentally killing his father. He freed certain Trojan descendants from captivity in Greece

From Brutus descended the whole line of British kings, culminating eventually in the legendary King Arthur.

and sailed away to Britain, where he founded the city of Troia Nova (New Troy), a name later corrupted to Trinovantum and then replaced by London. From Brutus descended the whole line of British kings, culminating eventually in the legendary King Arthur.

The tale of New Troy

This story first appears in the *British History* written by the Welsh antiquarian Nennius in the ninth century A.D. For the most part, Nennius' material on Aeneas seems to come from Virgil, although none of the Roman writers mentions Aeneas' great-grandson Brutus. The tale of Brutus received a much fuller treatment by Geoffrey of Monmouth in his *History of the Kings of Britain* (*c*.1135). What Virgil had accomplished for Aeneas, Geoffrey of Monmouth did for Brutus, and the descent of the British race from Brutus' Trojans was accepted as historical fact at least until Elizabethan times.

As the Romans had before them, the Britons created a glorious past for themselves, drawing on the legends of Aeneas and Brutus respectively. Many European kings did likewise, and the first European king to claim Trojan descent was the Holy

Roman Emperor and king of the Franks, Charlemagne, in the eighth century A.D. Throughout Europe the rule and laws of the emperor Charlemagne were imitated by many Saxon kings who had close links with his dynasty through the Church.

The Normans and the Danes also claimed Trojan descent. In Norse mythology the gods were said to have come from Troy. The story appears in the *Edda*, a collection of Norse traditions written by the Icelander Snorri Sturluson (1179–1241). Snorri relates that the Norse gods, the Aesir, first came from Asia and their home, Asgard, was Troy. The story of Ragnarok, which is found in *The Twilight of the Gods*, and tells how Asgard was overthrown and the world destroyed, is said to refer to the Trojan War. Snorri said that an old title of the god Thor, Oku-Thor, was a corruption of the Trojan Hector, and other links were drawn between Norse and classical myths.

The Norse tradition

Snorri's account is confused and refers to two journeys from Troy to Europe, the first by Oku-Thor, the second by his distant descendant Odin. Odin is said to have led his people to Denmark, Norway, and Sweden, where he built a city, Sigtunir, which was modeled on Troy. He is called the founding father of the Norse nations and in later times, Snorri further suggests, Odin and his companions were deified as Norse gods.

What really happened to any possible survivors of the Trojan War, if it ever took place, is hard to tell. However, in one sense the Trojans have survived. They live on in the European tradition as heroes, keeping alive the memory of a noble city.

Troy-town maze
One of the few surviving turf-cut mazes in Britain can be seen at Troy Farm, in Oxfordshire.

TROJAN GAMES
A number of turf-cut mazes, called Troy-towns, are still to be found in Britain. According to folklore, the Trojan Brutus, legendary founder of Britain, introduced a military maneuver called the Game of Troy, and the pattern of these mazes closely follows the pattern marked out by the exercise.

In the *Aeneid*, the epic story of the founding of Rome, the Roman poet Virgil describes Roman soldiers executing this same parade-ground cavalry maneuver.

Pattern of the labyrinth
For Virgil, the Game of Troy provided a link between Troy and Rome. The pattern of the maneuver closely matched that of the labyrinth, built by the legendary King Minos at Knossos, on the Greek island of Crete, to conceal the half-man, half-bull creature known as the Minotaur. According to Virgil, it was the Cretans who first settled in Troy. And their game was brought by Aeneas to Rome.

The link with Britain is even more tenuous. However, a maze design found on Cretan coins is identical to some of the British Troy-town mazes.

Norse god
This first-centuy B.C. statue of the Viking god Odin is from Denmark.

THE VANISHING ANASAZI

A mysterious American people who came from nowhere and vanished just as mysteriously, the Anasazi left buildings and roads as monuments to their existence.

ABOUT 1,000 YEARS AGO in the Four Corners area where the modern states of New Mexico, Arizona, Utah, and Colorado meet, an American Indian culture called the Anasazi emerged out of scattered bands of seminomadic hunter-gatherers. These bands had inhabited the southwest for thousands of years and formed the dominant cultural group. They gradually developed permanent settlements, a fairly complex civilization, and sophisticated methods of farming.

Cliff dwellers
Sizable Anasazi settlements have been found built into the recesses of canyon walls, such as Cliff Palace at Mesa Verde, Colorado.

Log, brush, and mud pits

Archeologists have established that the early Anasazi lived in dwellings called pithouses, which were made of logs, brush, and mud set into pits. They wove fine baskets, which provided the archeological name for this stage of their development: Basket Maker. Between A.D. 450 and 700, the Anasazi also appear to have began to develop the skill of pottery making. The pithouse type of structure later became adapted into circular, semi-subterranean ritual chambers, which were called kivas.

In the eighth century A.D., the Anasazi first began to construct rectangular houses. Flat-roofed and made of mud, rock, and posts, these dwellings were built in groups, which were called pueblos (meaning "towns") by the early Spaniards.

Researchers believe that there were four branches of Anasazi culture — the Mesa Verde peoples in southwest

> **The Anasazi gradually developed permanent settlements, a fairly complex civilization, and sophisticated methods of farming.**

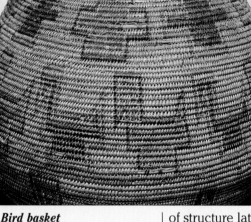

Bird basket
The Anasazi were famed for their basket making. This coiled basket with a bird design, dating from about A.D. 700, was woven from fiber taken from the yucca plant. It was made by the Mesa Verde peoples of southwest Colorado.

Anasazi Great House
The remains of a Great House at Pueblo Bonito in Chaco Canyon demonstrate the building skills of the Anasazi.

Colorado and southeast Utah, the Kayenta group in northeastern Arizona, the Virgin culture in southwestern Utah, and the peoples located around Chaco Canyon in northwestern New Mexico. This last branch appears to have been the key group, and so distinctive was the Anasazi flowering there that the term *Chacoan* is often used to describe the whole culture. Archeological studies have revealed the existence of a group of communities in and around Chaco Canyon that functioned as a highly integrated society.

Spiral design
By about A.D. 1100, Anasazi pottery was fired, then polished and painted. Each settlement appears to have developed different designs. This pitcher is from Chaco Canyon, New Mexico.

Great kivas
Archeological evidence indicates that between A.D. 900 and 1115, the Chacoan pueblos began to develop into multi-storied and terraced complexes, or Great Houses, with walls, courtyards, storage pits, and many kivas, including huge ceremonial chambers called Great Kivas. As well as monumental architecture, there were extensive manufacturing and trade systems, and complex canals and dams to manage the erratic and often limited water supply.

Evidence of Anasazi religious activity is seen not only in the kivas, but also in complex astronomical practices allied to ceremonial, and agricultural, needs. Some buildings seem oriented to specific sun positions, and rock paintings, also including astronomical themes, may mark the observing stations of the Anasazi sun-watcher priests.

Cannibal culture?
The archeologist Paul Nickens runs a Colorado-based consultancy investigating the Anasazi burial sites. These sites apparently contain evidence of cannibalism. He suggests that it could have been a scarcity of water and game that forced the Indians to prey on their neighbors. This could be seen as a symptom of the decline of their culture. This theory is reinforced by Nickens's observation that the victims' remains appear to have been treated with respect, as they were placed in neat piles in ceremonial rooms.

The Anasazi culture suddenly disappeared about A.D. 1300. No one knows for certain why this happened, but it was probably due to drought and the resulting loss of resources and breakdown in social cooperation among the various groups. After abandoning their centers, it appears likely that the Anasazi melted back into the vast landscapes of the southwest, becoming the ancestors of today's Pueblo Indians.

Cotton shirt
Elaborate weaving, like this shirt made from cotton, was done by Anasazi men.

Mystery roads
Several Chaco roads converge at the site of an Anasazi Great House at Pueblo Alto, on the northern ridge of Chaco Canyon, New Mexico.

THE CHACO ROADS
The most enigmatic ceremonial feature left by the Chacoan Anasazi is the 600-mile system of roads that radiate in all directions from Chaco Canyon. They were well constructed, straight, and up to 10 yards wide.

Mysterious thoroughfares
Archeologists had difficulty in understanding why a people who had not invented the wheel and who had no horses needed such highly engineered thoroughfares. These roads link the ceremonial Great Houses with other shrine sites, and their straightness is uncanny. Douglas Preston, writing in *New Mexico Magazine* in September 1992, believes that the Chaco roads represent "one of the most powerful expressions of religious faith created by any peoples on this continent."

Far-flung evidence
Evidence of such roads has been found as far afield as southern Utah, where they can reach 16 1/2 yards in width. Archeologists suspect that there may well have been Chaco roads extending into all the Four Corner states. If this is true, then the apparently disparate groups of Anasazi may in fact have been one vast, inter-connected culture, spread over some 75,000 square miles.

MYSTERIES OF IMPERIAL CHINA

Twenty-two centuries ago, Shih Huang Ti, the mighty First Emperor of China, assembled a huge army. But all his soldiers were made of clay, and their barracks was a tomb.

Shih Huang Ti
Despite the magnificence of his tomb, the emperor's final journey was humiliating. He died while visiting the provinces. His ministers decided to return to the capital before revealing his death. The weather was hot and the body began to decompose, so the ministers bought a cartload of fish and carried it with them to disguise the smell.

IN 1974, WHILE DIGGING a well near Mount Li, in Shaanxi province, northern China, a group of peasants unexpectedly broke into an underground vault. As the diggers removed the red earth, they discovered, to their amazement, the heads of life-size terra-cotta figures. As they dug deeper, they uncovered an army of figures, drawn up in formation and facing east.

The first pit appeared to contain an infantry division of more than 3,000 men, with officers in chariots. As further excavations took place, a second pit was exposed, which contained a troop of cavalry, both horsemen and chariots, supported by archers. This pit contained some 1,400 figures, including men and horses. A third pit was uncovered, which appeared to represent the command headquarters of this terra-cotta army, with models of the general's chariot and 68 guardsmen. A fourth pit was empty.

The First Emperor's mausoleum

The peasants had inadvertently stumbled upon part of the great mausoleum of Shih Huang Ti, known as the First Emperor of China, who had died in 210 B.C. According to tradition, the First Emperor was known to have been buried close to Mount Li. The tomb mound, which

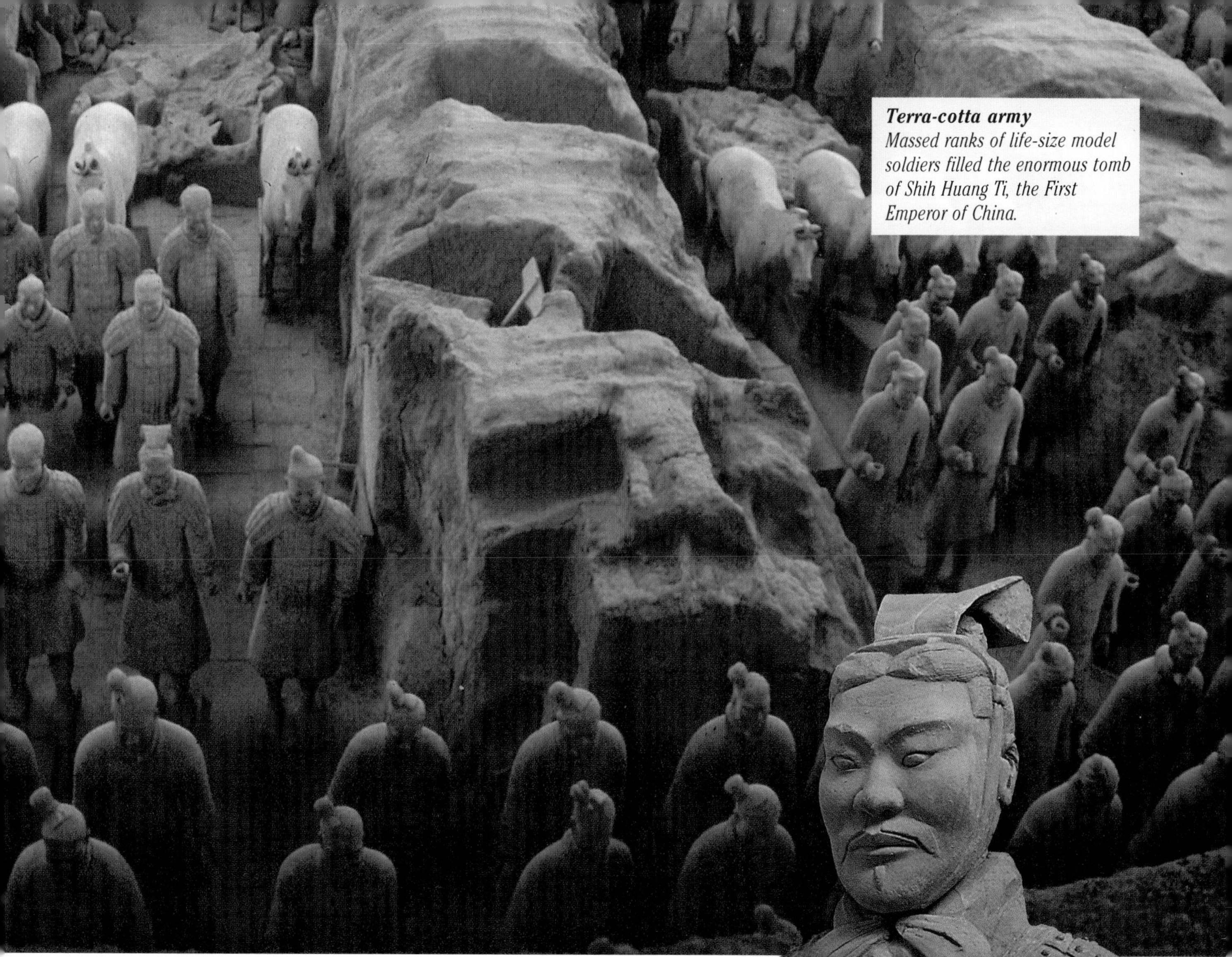

Terra-cotta army
Massed ranks of life-size model soldiers filled the enormous tomb of Shih Huang Ti, the First Emperor of China.

resembled a low hill, was a recognized feature but it had never been excavated.

The discovery of the terra-cotta army indicated the vast scale of the tomb. The army occupies an area of 3 acres, but archeologists suggest that the emperor may have built a "spirit city," so far undiscovered, over an area of 500 acres.

Army of individuals

The unmounted troops vary from lightly armed warriors to armored heavy infantry, and although there is some duplication in the manufacture of the bodies, every soldier has an individually modeled head with a recognizably different face. The figures could have been made from a rough mold and then the sculptors might have used fine clay to form details such as eyes, mouth, and nose. The statues seem to represent real people. Examination of the figures indicates that they were originally painted. It also appears that the warriors held real weapons. But most of the weapons seem to have been stolen at some time.

Although early rulers had claimed to have held sway over the whole of China, their domains were concentrated in the north of the country, and during the first millennium B.C.

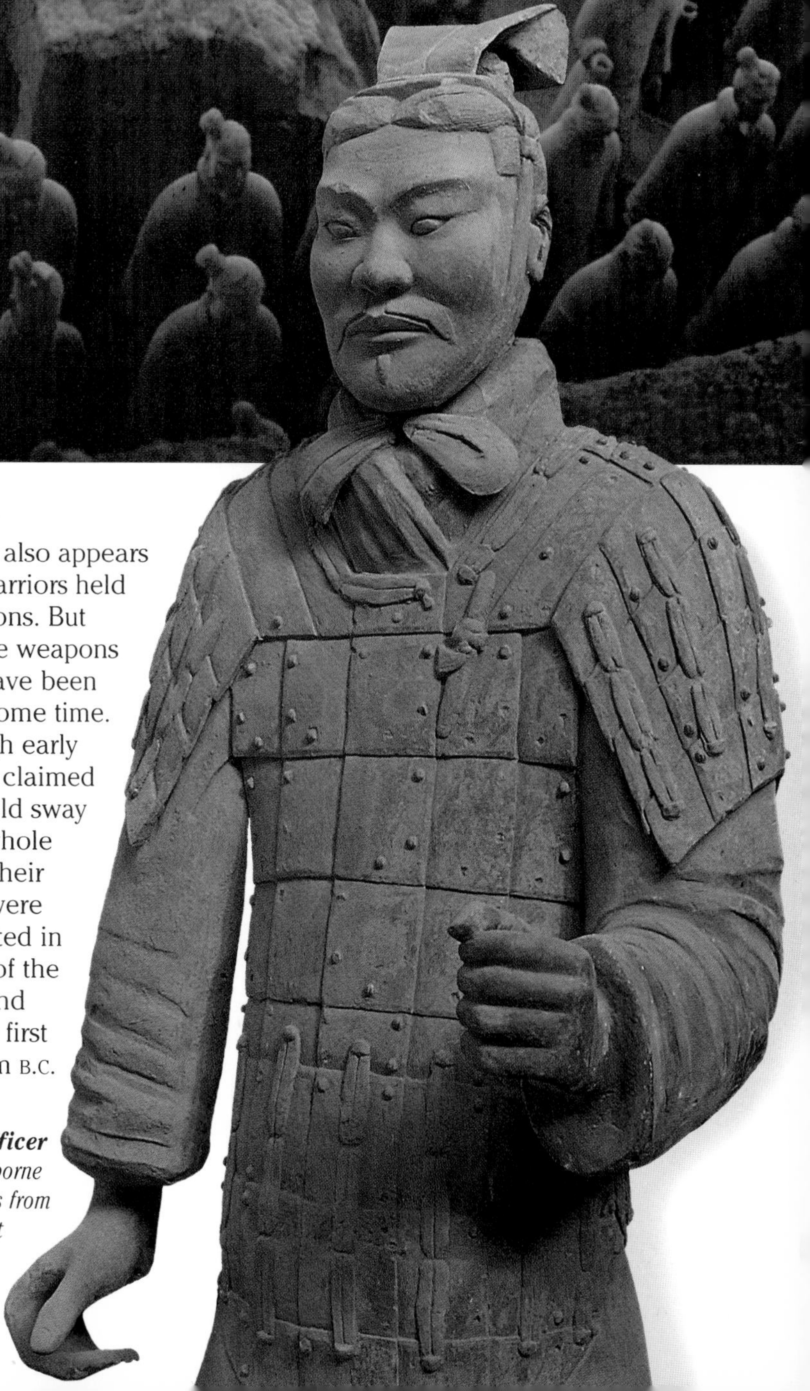

Armored officer
This chariot-borne commander is from the first pit at Mount Li.

the land was split up into a number of small kingdoms. Eventually the western realm of Ch'in conquered all the other kingdoms, and by 221 B.C. its empire spread over virtually the whole country.

The ruler of Ch'in became the First Emperor, Shih Huang Ti, who has been portrayed as both hero and villain. He was a great reformer, standardizing

> **The Great Wall can be seen as marking the northern edge of the land, in the same way as the sea to the east and south, and the mountains to the west. The Chinese believed that the civilized world ended at the Great Wall.**

weights, measures, and money; building roads, and revising the written language. In stark contrast to his reforming zeal, Shih Huang Ti was also notorious for his cruelty. He buried alive Confucian scholars who disagreed with him and burned their books. His autocratic rule was totally repressive, with heavy taxation and forced labor.

Holding back the Huns

Some of that forced labor was used by Shih Huang Ti to build the Great Wall. A number of short sections of wall had been built in previous centuries to stem incursions by the non-Chinese from the north and west. These people, regarded by the Chinese as savages, lived in what is now Mongolia and, when they finally migrated westward, became known to history as the Huns.

Shih Huang Ti renovated the fortified sections and joined them to make a defensive barrier running more than 1,500 miles across the north of China. Hundreds of

Footsoldier
This infantryman is from the tomb at Mount Li. His features are typical of the people of the Weihe Valley: square face, broad forehead, large mouth with thick lips, moustache and beard.

The Great Wall of China
The wall runs for 1,500 miles across the north of China. It was reconstructed in the 15th and 20th centuries.

thousands of men were forced to work on building the Great Wall, and thousands died before it was finished.

Apart from the Great Wall's obvious purpose in keeping out the non-Chinese, some historians have argued that it was also intended to keep the Chinese in. Moreover, according to Chinese philosophy, in order to obtain power over a territory, its borders first have to be defined. Therefore, the Great Wall can be seen as marking the northern edge of the land, in the same way as the sea to the east and south, and the mountains to the west. The Chinese believed that the civilized world ended at the Great Wall; anything beyond its boundaries might be conveniently forgotten.

Human sacrifice

It seems Shih Huang Ti was not satisfied with having conquered the whole of the known world, as he saw it; he wanted to take his army into the next world and conquer that as well. An earlier Chinese burial custom was for servants and wives

TOMB OF THE EMPEROR

A description of the mausoleum interior was left by the historian Ssuma Ch'ien, who wrote in the first century B.C. The coffin itself is said to have been cast in copper, and the tomb was filled with treasure and precious stones. Automatically firing crossbows were rigged up to shoot any thief who might break in, while those who had worked on the interior and knew its secrets were killed. Trees and grass were planted over the mausoleum to make it seem like an ordinary hill.

The world in miniature

The tomb is reported to have contained a model of the world. The stars were represented above, possibly painted on the ceiling, although Ssuma Ch'ien does not make this clear, and the provinces of China were modeled below. All the country's streams, including the Huang He River and the Jinsha Jiang River, were reproduced with mercury and flowed into a miniature ocean. There were also models of pavilions, palaces, and offices.

World power

Something more than simple greed or egotism probably underlies the First Emperor's model of the world. In China at that time it was believed that the microcosm and the macrocosm were intimately and magically connected. It was considered a treasonable offence for anyone but the emperor to own a map; because to own a map also created the possibility of magically controlling the very territory it represented. In modeling the earth within his tomb, then, it is possible that the First Emperor believed he could still control the world even after his death.

to follow the dead ruler to the tomb as human sacrifices, to serve him in the next world. The afterlife was known as the Yellow Springs, and was thought to be largely a duplicate of this world. Before Shih Huang Ti's time, it had become customary to substitute figurines for human corpses. Nothing, however, has been found to match the size of the First Emperor's clay army.

Even before he had established his empire, Shih Huang Ti had begun to work on his tomb, which was far larger and more magnificent than anything seen before. The forced labor used to build this structure alone amounted to 700,000 men.

Awaiting excavation

The site of the burial mound has always been a well-known local landmark, but such is the enormous backlog of Chinese archeological work that there are no plans to excavate the

First Emperor's awesome tomb before the beginnning of the 21st century.

The design of traditional Chinese walled cities shows a similar concern for duplicating the world. The cities were always aligned to the cardinal points, and the walls were square in layout, to match the shape of the earth, which was believed to be square. The city represented the world in microcosm and was magically connected with it. If good government and order could be

Horse-drawn chariots
The horses, chariots, and drivers shown being care-fully excavated here are made of bronze.

fire, which held sway over the south; at the same time, the northern gate would be opened to allow access to the elemental influence of water.

At the start of the 15th century A.D. the Ming dynasty emperor Ch'eng Tsu (also known as the Yung-lo emperor) made up his mind to build his capital at Beijing. But there, as well as the city representing a microcosm, it also represented the figure of a god.

Before Ch'eng Tsu began building his city, the area round Beijing was known as the Bitter Sea Waste, which may refer to the fact that the local water sources are naturally brackish. It seems likely that half a million years ago the area was actually under the sea. And in Chinese thought, water was very much the province of dragons. The man given the responsibility for planning the city of Beijing was an imperial adviser, Liu Bowen, about whom a number of stories have sprung up. According to one, Liu Bowen was concerned that the local dragons would resent him building a city on their territory, and he therefore had to take measures to subdue them. His idea was to represent the body of the dragon-slaying god Nezha in the construction of the city itself.

Heavily armed god

Nezha was an imported god of Indian origin, usually shown as a young boy with eight arms, riding on fiery wheels. Each of his hands held a different weapon. Soon after he was born he killed the son of the Dragon King of the Eastern Sea. As a penance, he committed suicide, but he was later reborn from a lotus flower. Whether or not we believe the story that Nezha appeared to Liu Bowen in a vision and told him to copy his body in the design of the city, the

Imperial scale

The large building dominating the courtyard of the Forbidden City, Beijing, is the Hall of Supreme Harmony. It was the principal audience chamber, which formed the center of the palace. The Forbidden City was the imperial palace, which was inhabited by one adult male only, the emperor himself, along with his young sons, the empress, concubines, women attendants, and eunuchs.

established within the microcosm of the city walls, this influence would then spread out and resonate throughout the surrounding countryside. Similarly, magic could be worked with the city itself. In times of drought in the country, the southern gate would be closed, in an attempt to alleviate the problem by blocking off the influence of the element

Grand throne

The throne hall in the Hall of Supreme Harmony in the Forbidden City, Beijing. Visitors passed their messages to an official at the bottom of the steps, and he relayed them to the emperor seated above.

god's presence there was thought not only to subdue the dragon, but also to provide a guardian deity with associations of immortality and rebirth. The implication was that, no matter what happened, Beijing would always rise again as an eternal city. With the capital guarded in this way, Nezha's protection would then extend to the entire country.

Anatomy of the city

The walls and gates of the main city represented the outer extremities of Nezha's body. There were eleven gates: eight of these gates represented his hands, two his feet, and the central southern gate his head. The Imperial City, at the center of Beijing, contained his body, while the streets represented his ribs. The buildings of the palace itself, the Forbidden City,

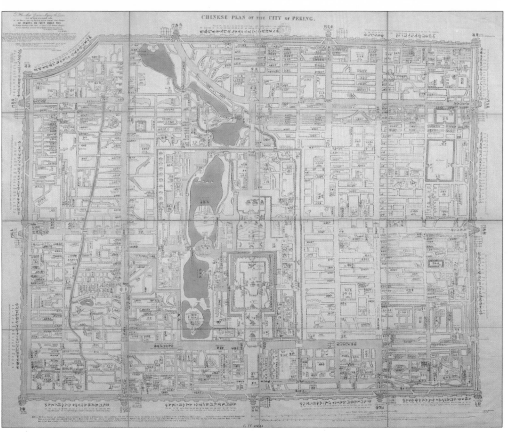

including wells representing his eyes, sewers his intestines, and so on.

Sadly, since the Communist revolution of 1949, much of Beijing has been torn down and rebuilt. The city walls have been destroyed, as have many of the 11 gates, though the Forbidden City, of course, remains. Some might think that it is a bad omen for the god Nezha, the city's protector, to be so neglected.

City plan
This plan of Beijing, dating from 1843, shows the Forbidden City at the center and the Imperial City, which was reserved for official residences, as a larger rectangle enclosing it. The design of the outer city represented the body of the dragon-slaying god Nezha.

The walls and gates of the main city represented the outer extremities of Nezha's body. There were eleven gates: eight of these represented his hands, two his feet, and the central southern gate his head.

---

symbolized the god's internal organs, while his spine and windpipe were shown by the Imperial Way, which ran northward through all of these. The numerous correspondences were very detailed, running to more than 30 in all,

Bronze lion
This beast is an example of the impressive bronze statuary in the Forbidden City, at the center of Beijing.

EASTER ISLAND

On the remote Pacific outcrop of Easter Island, hundreds of huge statues were carved using nothing more than Stone Age implements. Where the islanders came from and why they erected their monuments remain a mystery.

WHEN THE FIRST EUROPEAN sailors discovered Easter Island in 1722, there was little left of its once sophisticated culture. There were only a few thousand inhabitants, made up of 10 warring tribes, and a number of huge, enigmatic statues. In the decades that followed, the decline continued, reaching a low point in 1862, when most of the population was carried off by Peruvian slave traders. By the 20th century, when questions first began to be asked about the island's many unexplained mysteries, the answers seemed to have been lost forever.

Although there has been wild speculation that Easter Island might be a surviving remnant of a mythical lost continent such as Mu or Lemuria, there is no convincing evidence to suggest that it was inhabited before

When the first Europeans discovered Easter Island in 1722, there were only a few thousand inhabitants and a number of huge, enigmatic statues.

about A.D. 400. At that time Easter Island, which appears to be roughly triangular in shape and is only 15 miles long, appears to have been densely wooded. It is now virtually treeless, and anthropologists speculate that overpopulation and the resulting deforestation were the main factors in the society's collapse.

From east or west?
Easter Island is one of the most isolated spots on the planet. Its nearest neighbor, 1,200 miles to the west, is Pitcairn Island (where in 1790 mutineers from the British naval ship H.M.S. *Bounty* sought refuge on the uninhabited island), while the coast of South America lies 2,000 miles to the east. Wherever they came from, the original Easter Islanders would have had to have been astonishingly proficient sailors.

Norwegian explorer and scientist Thor Heyerdahl believed that the Polynesian Islands in the Pacific were colonized by sailors from Peru. His famous Kon-Tiki expedition of 1947 proved successfully that, using balsa-

wood rafts, Peruvian navigators could have reached the Polynesian Islands by sailing some 5,000 miles from the western coast of South America to the islands east of Tahiti. Eight years later Heyerdahl mounted another expedition, this time to Easter Island. Heyerdahl noted some cultural similarities between the island and the Americas. He saw, for example, that a type of reed, the *totora*, which grows on Easter Island, is usually found only on the South American continent. He concluded that Easter Island, like the Polynesian Islands, had been colonized from Peru.

Thor Heyerdahl

In spite of the great popular appeal of Thor Heyerdahl's well-publicized expeditions and theories, he has failed to convince the academic establishment that the original Easter Islanders and Polynesians came from Peru.

Source of mystery

The Easter Islanders are clearly Polynesian peoples — their language shares the same characteristics as the other island languages far to the west — and the Polynesians were known to be adventurous sailors, whereas there is little to indicate that the ancient peoples of South America ever developed any great interest in navigation. Perhaps the origins of the first inhabitants of Easter Island will always remain a mystery. But, wherever they came from, it is certain that this isolated people developed a unique and fascinating culture.

Volcanic rock

Statue carving on Easter Island is thought to have begun about A.D. 1100 and seems to have continued until civil wars broke out in the 1680's. The statues were carved from volcanic tufa, which can be softened with water in its natural state, making it easier to cut, but which hardens later when freed from the

Island guardian?
The Easter Island statues, called moai *in the local language, were positioned so that they looked inland, away from the sea.*

Cutting edges
These ancient stone tools are from Easter Island.

THE STONES THAT WALK
In 1986 an experiment carried out by Norwegian explorer and scientist Thor Heyerdahl seemed to suggest that the local islanders' legendary belief that the Easter Island statues walked to their location on their *ahu* platforms may in fact be correct. Under Heyerdahl's direction 20 islanders moved a 13-foot tall, 8-ton statue using only four ropes.

Slow progress
Two ropes were attached to the head of the upright statue, two near the base. While one team of men using the upper ropes tilted the statue to the right, another team pulled the left of the base forward several inches. Then the statue was tilted to the left and the right of the base advanced. In this way the statue could be described as "walking" six yards in an hour. This may seem slow progress, but it shows that it is possible to move the statues with remarkably few laborers.

inactive volcanoes, but only one, Rano Raraku, appears to have been used for quarrying the statues. Each statue seems to have been carved in a single piece, using basalt picks, by excavating the stone around it until the horizontal figure was complete. Even though the greatest emphasis was placed on the head, the statues were carved to show the limbs and body at least in basic form. Later the statues were provided with separate hats, or top knots, carved in red stone from the southern part of the island, near the Rana Kao volcano.

Stone platforms
From the quarry, the statues were moved to stone platforms, called *ahu*, most of which were situated around the island's coasts. Some 600 statues were set up in this way, although many more remained abandoned or incomplete on the slopes of Rano Raraku. They were generally between 6 and 16 feet tall, though some of the larger ones reached 30 feet, and one, left half-carved, would have been an enormous 65 feet tall.

How the statues were moved from the quarry to their platforms was a mystery that puzzled investigators for many years. One theory suggested that they were moved on log rollers and that this over-use of wood finally led to deforestation and the collapse of the society. However, the islanders had a much simpler explanation: According to legend the statues simply walked to their destination.

Earthbound statue
This statue was never completed and remains, partially carved, on the slopes of the extinct volcano Rano Raraku.

The *ahu* platforms, the final destination of the statues, were raised higher at their seaward edge and then sloped away inland, and they are believed to have been connected with the disposal of the dead. A body would be placed on the platform wrapped in a blanket of bark and left to decompose until only the bones remained. These could then be buried in chambers within the *ahu* or elsewhere.

The accepted explanation of the statues is that they were representations of the notable dead, either clan chiefs or other important personages.

The generally accepted explanation of the purpose of the statues is that they were representations of the notable dead, either clan chiefs or other important personages. The statues were positioned on the *ahu* so that they looked inland, away from the sea, and anthropologists have suggested that apart from being memorials they also signified that the dead chief was still present and over-seeing the fortunes of the tribal lands.

Ten tribes
The island population was divided into 10 tribes, and it is believed that there was a certain amount of competition among them to build larger and more impressive

statues than their neighbors. This form of competition appears to have diverted the energies that might otherwise have been devoted to warfare, and kept the island relatively peaceful throughout the entire statue-building period. When the civil wars did eventually break out, one strategy was to attack the other clans' *ahu* and overthrow their statues, thereby depriving the opposing clan of their ancestors' goodwill.

Bright influence

Another possible explanation for the statues' location was first pointed out by the American archeologist William Mulloy. He suggested that they may be aligned to significant points in the solar calendar. In 1965 Mulloy investigated the positioning of 272 *ahu* and found suggestive solar orientations for 45 of them. This result, however, is little more than would be expected from chance.

Further investigations conducted in 1987 by the Harvard astronomer William Liller and the Chilean meteorologist Julio Duarte on three or four major monuments appear to indicate that they are aligned with important solar rising points on the horizon and with the cardinal points. One of these statues, Rua Tau Ra'a, aligns with a small island

directly to the east, whose name means "island pointing at the red sun."

So far the alignments seem to refer only to the sun, with nothing to suggest an interest in the moon, planets, or stars, but local rock art includes numerous representations of lunar crescents, constellations, and comets. This astronomical theory need not invalidate former theories about the *ahu* and the statues, but it does add an extra dimension to them. And in times to come, who knows what other mysteries the Easter Island statues may reveal?

Somber sentries
Some researchers believe that the positioning of the Easter Island statues may be related to points on the horizon that are significant in the solar calendar.

COLOSSAL STATUES

On the coast of Brittany, in western France, not far from the ancient megalithic remains of Carnac, a massive, 350-ton, 75-foot-tall granite obelisk once stood. It fell and broke into large fragments during an earthquake in 1722. Archeologists believe that this great pillar was constructed about 2000 B.C. to represent the guardian spirit of the land.

Later, in southern Europe, sculptors became more skilled, and began to create vast statues to represent the gods. In ancient Greece, these towering figures, known as colossi, were often placed in temples.

In the fifth century B.C., Phidias, the most celebrated Greek sculptor, created the enormous statue of Zeus, seated on a throne, at Olympia in southern Greece. He also constructed the giant statue of the goddess Athena, which stood in the Acropolis in Athens.

Roman colossi

The ancient Romans built giant statues as well. On the Capitol in Rome stood a statue of Jupiter, and in the Palatine Library, a huge bronze statue of Apollo.

According to the Roman historian Pliny the Elder, writing in the first century A.D., the most outstanding giant statue was that of the Roman god Mercury,

which was erected on a mountaintop in the Auvergne region, central France.

In the 19th century, the French sculptor F. A. Bartholdi planned to recreate this colossus, but he could not raise the necessary funds. He had to content himself with a 151-foot-tall statue. In 1886 Bartholdi's statue was presented to the people of America by the people of France. This is the Statue of Liberty, which stands in New York harbor.

Gigantic digit
The hand belonging to the 40-foot-tall colossus of the Roman emperor Constantine, which once stood near the Colosseum in Rome.

CHAPTER FIVE

GENIUS OF THE PAST

Technology has advanced rapidly in recent centuries. Yet ancient man was an innovator as well, and many ingenious inventions — for example, the steam engine and the drainage pump — are older than you might imagine.

When asked what is the most important invention of all time, most people would answer: the wheel. And many experts would agree. Its earliest known use dates from 3500 B.C. in Mesopotamia, the land that lay between the Euphrates and Tigris rivers that is now known as Iraq. Potters are credited with the invention, through their discovery that wet clay could be more easily shaped with the hands if it was placed on a spinning turntable. (Part of one such potter's wheel, dating from 3250 B.C., has been found on the site of

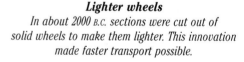

Early transportation
Wheels were originally made from solid sections of wood cut from tree trunks. They were primarily used on man-drawn carts to make the transportation of heavy or bulky objects easier.

Prototype chariot
A four-wheeled chariot (below) is painted on stone in the tombs of the Mesopotamian kings of Ur, in present-day Iraq. The wheels appear to be made of two planks of wood joined together. This depiction dates from about 2500 B.C.

Plank wheel
Wheels made from a number of planks of wood strengthened with crosspieces were found to be much stronger than solid sections of logs.

the ancient Mesopotamian city of Ur.) A circular turntable could be spun if it was placed on an axle that was kept upright in a hole in the ground.

Before the development of the wheel, heavy objects were moved on sledges, or by means of rollers, most often tree trunks. Archeologists believe that about the time that potters were first using wheels, crude wheels were also being used for transport. Early wheels were probably constructed by cutting a cross section from a log. Wheels made in this way soon split, and so a band of metal was tightened around the edge to hold the wheel together. It is believed these wheels were attached to the sledges that had been used earlier for drawing loads.

Revolutionary wheel
By 3200 B.C., solid wheels were made by joining planks until they formed a square; this square was then hacked into a circle and strengthened by attaching wooden, or metal, crosspieces. The wheel was made more durable with the addition of a band of metal hammered around the edge. Wheelwrights then found that they could make a turning axle by attaching it to the underside of the cart, or plow, with leather straps or metal bands. It seems that the wheels were attached rigidly to the ends of the axles and thus turned together with them. Four-wheeled carts revolutionized the business of transporting heavy loads. And two wheels on an axle attached to a plow facilitated the plowing of land for planting crops.

In addition, wheelwrights soon discovered that by leaving a small gap between the axle and the center of the wheel, the wheel might be made to turn more smoothly. They also discovered that they could reduce friction by plugging this gap with short, cylindrical pegs, thus effectively creating the first roller bearings.

There are differing opinions among experts about where the first wheeled vehicles originated. Some archeologists argue that they came from Mesopotamia, while others suggest that they originated on the steppes of central Asia, where the flat, open terrain would be more suited to the design of the early four-wheeled carts. However, the discovery of ancient carts in places as far apart as western Europe,

Lighter wheels
In about 2000 B.C. sections were cut out of solid wheels to make them lighter. This innovation made faster transport possible.

Egypt, India, and China suggests to archeologists that the wheel was invented in more than one location. The late Jacob Bronowski, in his formidable survey of early civilization, *The Ascent of Man* (1973), argued that "the wheel and the axle become the double root from which invention grows."

Riding on horseback
Soon enough, a new development accelerated the rate of change. By about 2000 B.C. people had begun riding on horseback, no longer using the horse solely as a beast of burden. At this time the cumbersome early wheels evolved

Stone wheel
In parts of the world where trees were scarce, such as China and Turkey, wheels were made of stone.

into spoked wheels. These lighter wheels were made by cutting away large sections of the inner wheel and then strengthening it with struts or crossbars. Ultimately, the result of these developments was the creation of the fast, light chariot, which became civilization's first decisive war machine. When, for example, knife blades were fixed to the chariot wheels, they became formidable weapons.

Minoan technology

Soon after the first light horse-drawn chariots had been developed in the Middle East, a rich trading civilization arose on the Mediterranean island of Crete, with its capital at Knossos. Archeologists have established that earlier settlements there had been destroyed by an earthquake some 3,700 years ago. The city and palace were rebuilt on a grand scale by King Minos, who is said to have created the famous labyrinth for the Minotaur, a legendary creature who was half-man and half-bull.

The Minoans became the conquerors of the Mediterranean. Their fleet was so great that the palace at Knossos had no need of walls to defend it. When the British archeologist Sir Arthur Evans began excavating the palace of Minos in 1900, he found its corridors so confusing that he suspected it might be the source of the story of the labyrinth.

The ruins revealed that the palace of Minos had an advanced system of plumbing and drainage. Surface water was carried away by covered drains, and skillfully jointed clay water pipes. Beside the magnificent throne room, with its wall paintings of youths and maidens vaulting over the backs of bulls, there was the queen's bathroom, and, at the end of the corridor, one of the first flush toilets known to history, with water brought down from the roof in pipes. Water pitchers found nearby suggested that the toilet was flushed by pouring water down it, while odors were prevented from rising from the sewers underneath by means of a stone plug.

Disappearing civilization

The Minoan civilization appears to have vanished abruptly about 1450 B.C. From contemporary records archeologists know that the volcano on the island of Santorini, north of Crete, erupted at about this time. They speculate that this may have caused a massive tidal wave that swept all life off the nearby islands. It seems probable that the Minoan fleet was destroyed, leaving the Minoans undefended, thereby allowing invaders from the Greek mainland to the north to pour into Crete. During the next four centuries hordes of barbarians, known as the Sea Peoples, brought both the Minoan and the early Greek civilization to the point of collapse.

About 800 B.C. the Greeks began to rebuild their civilization and their intellectual life. A man named Thales, a mathematician and astronomer who lived in the Greek colony of Miletus in Asia Minor (present-day Turkey), about 600 B.C., is held to be one of the world's first great scientists. He is credited with asking the question: Of what is the universe made? Thales also predicted the eclipse of the sun that stopped the battle between the Lydians and Medes on May 28, 585 B.C.

Great inventor

Foremost among ancient Greek inventors was Archimedes, who was born in about 287 B.C. in the city of Syracuse on the island of Sicily, southern Italy. As a young man, Archimedes went to study in Alexandria, Egypt, the center of learning in the ancient world. On his return to Syracuse, Archimedes joined the court of King Hieron, the ruler of Syracuse, for whom he produced a number of remarkable inventions.

One of his first engineering feats was the development of a pump for draining

> ## The ruins revealed that the palace of Minos had an advanced system of plumbing.

Regal bathroom
At the end of a corridor leading off the queen's bathroom in the palace of Minos at Knossos, Crete, archeologists found one of the first flush toilets.

Chariot wheel
Larger sections of wood were cut out of solid wheels as wheelwrights attempted to design lighter wheels. Struts or crossbars strengthened the wheel and these later developed into spokes.

THE PHAISTOS DISC

A small clay disc from Minoan Crete has baffled archeologists for decades. Beautifully worked, it bears writing in an unknown language.

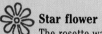

In 1908 A TEAM of Italian archeologists excavating the Minoan palace of Phaistos in southern Crete discovered a clay disc measuring 6½ inches in diameter and ¾ inch thick. A hieroglyphic text ran in a spiral pattern on both sides of the disc. Each character had been individually pressed into the clay. Archeologists believe that the disc is the earliest document to have been found that was printed from a set of seals, or dies.

Three different forms of writing existed in ancient Crete. These types — two thought to be in an undeciphered Minoan language and the third a form of archaic Greek — were usually made by marking clay tablets with a stylus. The characters on the Phaistos disc, with their finely drawn human figures, animals, boats, and other recognizable objects, resemble none of these scripts. Forty-five different signs are used on the disc, and over both sides the text has a total of 241 impressions, divided into 61 groups. Each group is separated by a line that appears to have been marked with a stylus.

Words in pictures

Archeologists suggest it is most likely that each sign stands for a single syllable, so each of the 61 groups would represent an individual word. Experts are not certain which way the characters should be read. Some

Side one of the Phaistos disc

108

suggest that the spiral runs from rim to center, while others believe the reverse. But all are agreed on which side is the front, and which is the back.

Some small markings near the rim suggest that the disc may only be pages four and five of a longer text. This would seem logical because the amount of work required to make the set of stamps would have been worthwhile only for a long document.

Origins and meanings

The disc was unlike anything previously found in Crete. At first archeologists considered that it must have been imported from somewhere else. A notable proponent of this argument was English archeologist Sir Arthur Evans, who began excavating the Minoan palace at Knossos in 1900. He believed that the disc might have originated from what is now southwestern Turkey. Other theories put forward are that the disc was made

by people as distant as the Philistines, Libyans, Semites, and Basques. However, other Cretan inscriptions have since been found that resemble the signs on the disc, making a Cretan origin for the disc more likely. Likewise a number of suggestions have been put forward to explain the purpose of the disc; these range from a magical amulet to an astronomical chart, from a hymn to a goddess to a list of soldiers.

In spite of all the problems, both professional and amateur archeologists have tried to translate the disc. None of the translations, however, has been convincing, and the attempts range from the dubious to the ludicrous. The frustrating reality is that a text of 241 characters does not provide enough raw material for linguists to work with.

Until more examples of the same script are discovered, the Phaistos disc is likely to remain what it is now: a very beautiful yet baffling puzzle.

Woman in short gown and skirt
This sign has been interpreted as a crude representation of a Minoan lady who appears to be wearing an unusual double skirt.

Fist wound round with leather bands
A form of boxing was practiced in Crete. This sign, showing a primitive form of boxing glove, is believed to be connected with contests held there.

Animal skin?
On the Mediterranean island of Cyprus this sign represented an ingot of copper. Cyprus was the main source of copper for Crete, which may explain this sign on the disc. Is it possible that Crete traded animal skins for copper?

Ship with arrow on prow
The outline of a ship is quite clear in this sign. The arrowlike point on the prow of the vessel has been interpreted as indicating that this is a war galley.

Captive
A figure with hands bound behind his back is thought by some to be a prisoner. The right side of the sign has been obliterated, leading other experts to suggest that the whole sign may show a figure carrying some object.

Pagoda-like building?
This sign is believed to represent a tomb or a building. Alternatively, it may symbolize an ornate palanquin, or litter, which the Minoans were known to use to transport their eminent citizens.

Side two of the Phaistos disc

Lifting water
The Archimedean screw was an ingenious device that enabled water to be raised from a low-lying river or canal with the minimum of effort. When the handle is turned, water works its way up inside the cylindrical case enclosing the screw.

marshland. Known as the Archimedean screw, this pump consisted of a long tube in the shape of a corkscrew, with a handle at the end. This was often enclosed in a cylindrical case. When the end was lowered into water, and the handle turned at the other end, the water rose up the corkscrew and flowed into a tank. This form of pump is still used in Egypt today for irrigation of crops.

Bathtime solution
The most famous of Archimedes' discoveries was made when King Hieron suspected that a goldsmith had introduced some silver into a crown that should have been made of solid gold.
Hieron commanded Archimedes to discover the truth, but only without damaging the king's crown. Archimedes puzzled over the problem for many days until the solution, so the story goes, came to him as he was lowering himself into a bath. As the water splashed over the sides, he suddenly realized that the volume of the displaced water was precisely that of an object lowered into it. Legend has it that Archimedes became so excited that he ran naked through the streets of Syracuse shouting *Eureka* (meaning "I have found it.")
Archimedes placed Hieron's crown in a tub brimful of water and measured the volume of water displaced. He then compared

Greek inventor
The genius of Archimedes inspired this portrait by the 17th-century Spanish artist José Ribera.

it with the quantity of water displaced by an equal weight of pure gold. The volume of water displaced by the crown was greater than that displaced by the gold. Archimedes explained that his experiment proved that the crown's volume was greater than that of the equivalent weight of pure gold. The crown therefore contained another, less dense metal. King Hieron had the cheating goldsmith executed.

Archimedes was also apparently the first to grasp the principle of the pulley. According to legend, he staged a spectacular demonstration of its power when he raised a fully loaded merchant ship from the harbor by pulling on the end of a rope. He also invented a winch that allowed him to pull a sailing ship up on to the beach by turning a handle.

In 214 B.C., the Romans attacked Syracuse, and Archimedes was placed in charge of the city's defense. He turned his knowledge of levers to good effect and invented a number of war machines. These included catapults that hurled huge blocks of stone at the Roman legions. On top of the city's sea walls he placed massive cranes that dropped blocks of stone on the Roman ships. He also constructed giant iron claws designed to grab the prows of the enemy ships, lift them out of the water, and so capsize them.

Archimedes' heat ray
According to the Roman historian Lucian of Samosata, the most formidable of Archimedes' inventions was a heat ray. It took the form of a giant curved mirror that could intensify the power of the sun's rays and redirect them at the Roman ships to set them on fire.

Despite all Archimedes' ingenious war machines, however, the Romans finally overcame the Greeks. They captured Syracuse by scaling a wall one night when the defenders were all drunk after a celebration. Archimedes was killed by a Roman soldier, so the story goes, as he scratched a geometrical problem in the sand with a stick.

Another Greek inventor who made outstanding discoveries was Ctesibius, a contemporary of Archimedes, who lived and worked in Alexandria during the third century B.C. The son of a barber, Ctesibius was said to have constructed an adjustable mirror that went up and down on a rope so that his father's customers could watch the progress of their shaves and haircuts. This device apparently worked by means of a counterweight being placed in a kind of elongated wooden box built of planks.

Piston and valve

Ctesibius noticed that when he raised the mirror quickly, a hissing noise was heard as the descending counterweight forced air out of the box. This observation inspired him to construct a tube, with a tightly fitting cylindrical plunger, and thus create the first piston. Next he added a flap that would open when air or water was forced out of it, but that would then close and stop water or air flowing back into it. In this way, he made the first valve.

During the first century A.D., the city of Alexandria produced another great scientist, Hero, whose most intriguing creation was a hollow sphere set on an axis with two bent rods sticking out of either side. When water inside a sealed pan was heated, the steam rose through the hollow pipes that formed the axis. The steam then hissed out through the bent rods attached to the sphere, causing it to revolve at a high speed. Hero called his invention the *aeolipile* and regarded it as a toy. But he had, in fact, converted heat into motion. Thus his aeolipile employed the same principle used by the English inventor George Stephenson when he built the

first steam locomotive in 1814. Another of Hero's inventions, which had an immediate and practical application in the ancient world, was a surveying instrument called a *dioptra*. It combined a theodolite (an instrument that measures horizontal and vertical angles and is used to survey accurately a large area of land) with a level, and proved a most useful tool for architects and surveyors.

Early vending machine

Hero was also credited with inventing the first vending machine, which stood outside the temple and sold a quantity of holy water in exchange for a coin. The weight of the coin, it appears, operated a simple mechanism.

Many historians argue that the great age of inventions ended with the Greeks. Nevertheless the ancient Romans contributed several revolutionary inventions. Thick strata of chocolate-red volcanic dust called pozzolana are found in the area around Pozzuoli, near Naples, and also around Rome. When Roman builders mixed the pozzolana with lime and water, it made a soft mortar that set with great rigidity, even beneath water. Builders used this mixture to bind bricks and stones. When they added gravel to the mixture they had created concrete, a completely new material, and one that was to revolutionize building. Concrete was used, for example, in the lower parts of the dome of the Pantheon and in the Colosseum in Rome. Such massive self-supporting structures would have been impossible to erect before the invention of concrete.

> Hero's aeolipile employed the same principle used by the English inventor George Stephenson when he built the first steam locomotive in 1814.

Playing with steam
Hero designed his steam engine purely as a plaything. Although he had discovered how to convert heat into motion, he did not develop any practical application for his invention.

Roman edifice
The dome of the Pantheon in Rome, built in A.D. 118–19 by the emperor Hadrian, shows the spectacular way in which Roman builders used concrete.

THE PIRI RE'IS MAP

Is it possible that a 16th-century Turkish map might prove that ancient navigators had discovered and charted the New World centuries before Christopher Columbus made landfall in 1492?

*I*N 1929 IN THE IMPERIAL PALACE in Istanbul, Turkey, an intriguing map was discovered. Drawn on parchment made from gazelle skin by the Turkish admiral Piri Re'is in 1513, the map appeared to show a remarkably accurate representation of the coastline of the Atlantic Ocean, overlaid with a baffling series of grid-like lines. Piri Re'is's footnotes on the map claimed that he had compiled it using about 20 old maps and 8 *Mappa Mundi* (meaning "world maps") as his source.

Most 16th-century maps showed the shape of the landmasses, but they were often wildly out of proportion.

The Piri Re'is chart was exceptionally accurate for its time. The majority of 16th-century maps showed the shape of the landmasses, but they were often wildly out of proportion. Lines of latitude were reasonably accurate, as they could be fixed by reference to the stars. But cartographers at that time did not possess the technology to find longitude accurately. This prevented

Atlantic outline
The Piri Re'is map seems to show the eastern shore of the New World and the western coasts of Africa and the Iberian peninsula. The map includes many charming illustrations of ships, fantastic people, and animals.

them from charting how far east and west a landmass fell, which resulted in any number of mistakes. The inaccuracy of 15th-century navigational skills, for example, led at least in part to Columbus's accidental discovery of the continent of America. Columbus had calculated that it should be possible to reach Asia by sailing westward across the Atlantic. He truly believed that this voyage would be shorter than following the usual south and east route around Africa. And so, using a 15th-century map (which is now lost) of the Atlantic, he set sail from Palos on the southern coast of Spain and mistakenly believed that he had reached Asia when he first sighted the Canary Islands.

Babylonian map
The earliest known map of the world is a clay tablet that was found in Iraq. It is believed to date from about 500 B.C.

Early navigators
Archeologists believe that the Phoenicians explored the Mediterranean between 1500 B.C. and 500 B.C. This bronze plaque depicts Phoenician merchants loading goods onto ships in the ancient city of Tyre, which is the present-day town of Sour in southern Lebanon.

Forgotten map
The Piri Re'is map had lain forgotten in the Topkapi Museum in Istanbul until, in 1956, it was brought to the notice of Charles Hapgood, a professor of the history of science at Keene State College in New Hampshire. In 1966 he published *Maps of the Ancient Sea Kings*, in which he set out his theory that the accuracy of the Piri Re'is map suggested that ancient navigators had charted the world before history began to be written.

The inaccuracy of 15th-century navigation led to Columbus's accidental discovery of America.

Hapgood's book was highly speculative, but it made fascinating reading. He had formulated his theory after studying hundreds of old maps. He had in fact discovered some maps that were reasonably accurate when compared with modern maps. He believed that the common link among these maps was that they were all based on compasslike grids known as *portolans* (meaning "from port to port"). These, Hapgood suggested, had been used by medieval mariners to chart the Black Sea and the Mediterranean accurately.

Trial and error
The Piri Re'is map shows five such portolans, and after a long process of trial and error Hapgood believed that he had discovered how Piri Re'is had used them to draw his map. He argued that the centers of all five portolans lie on the circumference of a circle, and that the center of this circle was the intersection of longitude 30° east, which passes through the city of Alexandria, in northern Egypt, and latitude 23 1/2° north, which is the Tropic of Cancer. Alexandria was the center of learning in the ancient world, and Piri Re'is claimed that some of the maps he used had come from there. Then Hapgood enlisted the assistance of the mathematician Richard W. Strachan at the Massachusetts Institute of Technology, who studied the five portolans on the Piri Re'is map and was able to calculate their exact locations. Hapgood redrew the Piri Re'is chart

using a modern grid and compared it against a modern-day map of the same geographical area to test its accuracy.

Antarctic outline

Hapgood found obvious errors. The Amazon River, for example, appeared twice, and 900 miles of South America's east coast had been omitted. He also discovered that the Piri Re'is map had left out Drake Passage, which divides Antarctica and South America. Antarctica, however, appeared to lie in roughly the correct location, and its outline matched that of the coast of Queen Maud Land, which lies beneath the Antarctic ice sheet. However, the latest geological research suggests that Antarctica has been covered with ice for 25 million years. The extent of Queen Maud Land was assumed to be an impenetrable mystery until 1949, when a Swedish-British-Norwegian expedition used the modern technology of depth-sounding equipment to chart the terrain hidden beneath the ice for the very first time.

Portolan map

Hapgood also drew attention to another map drawn using portolans by a cartographer named Oronteus Finaeus in 1531. This map indicated that Finaeus, too, had a surprisingly detailed knowledge of Antarctic geography.

Hapgood found that the overall shape of the continent was startlingly like that on a modern map. He pointed out that: "The position of the South Pole, nearly in the center of the continent, seemed about right. The mountains that skirted the coasts suggested the numerous ranges that have been discovered in Antarctica in recent years."

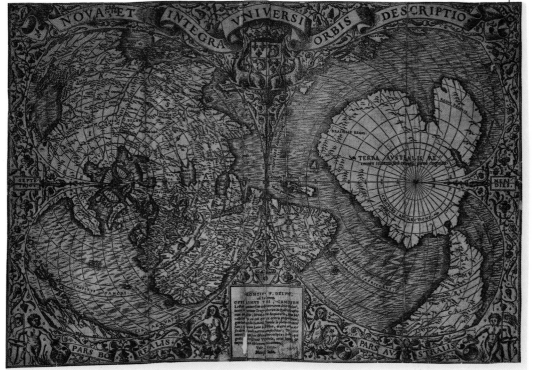

Hapgood claimed that maps drawn using portolans had to be based on maps far older than the oldest previously known, which date from 500 B.C. They seemed to point to some common source. The skill and knowledge shown by the people who had made these maps, he further claimed, were not equaled until the 18th century. Hapgood concluded that an advanced civilization had existed in remote times, before the rise of any known cultures. Hapgood decided to name this early civilization of explorers the Ancient Sea Kings. He argued that the skills of this civilization were lost and had to be re-discovered by later generations.

> Hapgood claimed that maps drawn using portolans had to be based on maps far older than the oldest previously known, which dates from 500 B.C.

Controversial theory

Hapgood's intriguing theory was greeted with skepticism by most experts. They attributed the uncanny accuracy of the Piri Re'is map to mere coincidence. Hapgood's controversial theory still has its supporters, but until archeological evidence is found to prove the existence of the civilization of the Ancient Sea Kings, his theories remain unproven.

World view
Map of the world, drawn by Oronteus Finaeus in 1531, shows Antarctica, seen on the right, in more accurate detail than might be expected from a 16th-century map.

Navigational aid
From the 12th century Western navigators used the lodestone to help determine a course. A needle was magnetized by stroking the lodestone (made of magnetic iron oxide). When hung on a string, the needle would point north.

UNBELIEVABLE INVENTIONS?

Could the ancients have developed the technology to produce electricity, computers, batteries, or even nuclear power? A number of archeological discoveries have caused some respected modern scholars to suggest that they did.

BAGHDAD BATTERY

The German archeologist Prof. Wilhelm Konig was in charge of Iraq's Museum Laboratory in Baghdad in June 1936, when railway construction workers nearby found an ancient grave covered with a stone slab. In it were many artifacts which dated it to the middle of the third century B.C.

Puzzling objects

One of the most puzzling objects in the grave, however, was a copper cylinder containing an iron rod. It looked very like a primitive battery. Prof. Konig had seen some other cylinders and rods from Iraq in the Berlin Museum, and when he returned he studied these carefully. He concluded that they were simple batteries that had been joined in series for electroplating gold and silver jewelry. Prof. Konig believed that the ancients had access to a level of technology previously thought to be exclusively modern.

The original Baghdad battery
The battery was found in an ancient grave near Baghdad in June 1936.

No one paid much attention to this amazing speculation because it seemed so unlikely that electricity had been discovered two and a half centuries before Christ. Yet when Walter Winton, of the London Science Museum, saw the artifact in 1962, he too immediately thought it was a battery. Subsequent experiments with replicas showed that a small current could be generated between the copper cylinder and the iron rod for as long as 18 days.

Shining example

The Egyptologist Dr. Arne Eggebrecht from Hildesheim in Germany made a replica of the Baghdad battery to illustrate how it might have been used to gild metal ornaments. Dr. Eggebrecht suspended a silver figurine in a gold solution and applied a current from the replica battery for 30 minutes. As a result the lower half of the figurine was coated in a thin layer of gold.

Light in the tombs

There is much speculation as to how artists managed to decorate the walls in the depths of ancient Egyptian tombs.

Why, say, are there elaborate wall paintings, yet no sign of the carbon that would drift upward from an oil lamp? One solution is that the wall paintings may have

Colorful tomb

This photograph of the tomb of Nefertari, wife of Ramses II, in the Valley of the Queens, Egypt, shows how intricate and brightly colored Egyptian tomb decorations were.

been done by daylight while the tomb was under construction. However, this seems an unlikely procedure since it would have seriously delayed the building work. Therefore the artists must have used some form of lighting that did not involve naked flames.

Is it possible that the Egyptians might have used battery-powered lights? In the great sandstone temple at Dandara, 30 miles north of the city of Luxor, there are wall engravings that look like electric lights and insulators. Some experts have suggested that this apparently unlikely solution could be the answer to yet another Egyptian puzzle.

Antikythera computer

In 1900 a sponge diver off the coast of the little Greek island of Antikythera found the wreck of an ancient ship, which sank about 65 B.C. with a cargo of wine amphorae, statues, and other artifacts. The oddest of these was a scientific instrument with cogged wheels. Careful cleaning revealed gears and inscriptions. In 1959 an English-born scholar, Prof. Derek J. de Solla Price of Yale University, announced that, as a result of his studies, he was convinced it was a kind of ancient Greek computer, and that its purpose was to determine the altitude of the sun, moon, and other celestial bodies.

His colleagues dismissed this as a fairy tale. However, in 1971, he subjected the "computer" to gamma radiography. This reportedly revealed more details of gears — 30 of them. This made Prof. de Solla Price even more certain that the mechanism was an early computer.

Heavenly device

This extraordinary mechanism was discovered among the artifacts aboard the wreck of an ancient Greek cargo ship. Experts now agree that it is a computer. It shows the movements of heavenly bodies in relation to one another.

George Sassoon and Rodney Dale

Illustrated by Martin Riches

The Lord gave the Israelites a nuclear-powered manna-producing machine which sustained them for forty years in the wilderness.

"I find it a bit frightening to know that just before the fall of their great civilization the ancient Greeks had come so close to our age, not only in their thought but also in their scientific technology."

Prof. Derek J. de Solla Price, *Scientific American*

Ancient gearing

Prof. Derek J. de Solla Price created a reconstruction of the Antikythera computer (background image), which reveals the intricate workings of the ancient mechanism.

Golden sanctuary

Traditional belief holds that the Ark of the Covenant was a gold-plated wooden chest that housed the tablets of the law as given to Moses by God. Moses apparently constructed the Ark after seeing a fiery replica that descended from the heavens. The Bible tells how the Ark accompanied the Israelites during their wanderings in the wilderness. Its final resting place has never been discovered.

Nuclear nutrient

The electronics consultant George Sassoon and the biologist and engineer Rodney Dale introduced a highly controversial theory in their book, *The Manna Machine* (1978). They apparently reconstructed the Ark of the Covenant precisely as described in the Zohar, an ancient Jewish text. They concluded, however wildly, that the Ark, which accompanied Moses and his followers throughout their years in the wilderness, was in fact a complex and powerful nuclear device that was able to produce manna — the nourishing food that sustained the Israelites during their trek through the desert.

Illuminated image

The Ark of the Covenant as depicted in a 15th-century Bible.

PREHISTORIC FLIGHT

❧ *The art of flying seems to have been reinvented, more or less successfully, at different periods in history and in different locations around the globe.*

CCORDING TO HIS RECORDS, Archytas, a Greek scientist, made a working airplane, powered by a system of weights and compressed air, in the fourth century B.C. In earlier times, a guild of Greek artificers in India was famous for the construction of flying machines. An old Sanskrit text describes how one of the Greeks made a flying machine, described as a "mechanical rooster," and sold it to a rich Indian. He showed it to the king, who was jealous and demanded to know the secret of its construction. Faced with royal death threats, the owner of the rooster had, quite literally, to "fly" for his life.

Wooden puzzle

In 1898 excavators of an ancient Egyptian tomb at Sâqqara made a discovery that greatly puzzled them. It was a small wooden object with wings. Not knowing how to classify it, they put it in a box labeled "wooden bird models," and for years afterward it remained undisturbed in the basement of the Cairo Museum.

Ancient Egyptian craftsmen always made a small-scale model of the temple, ship, or whatever else they were planning to construct. Dr. Khalil Messiha is the leading expert on these models. In 1971 he was looking through the neglected boxes in the museum's basement and came across the little winged object. He thought at once that it might be a model airplane. At first he suspected a hoax, but examination by a number of specialists confirmed it as a genuine artifact, made about 200 B.C. The Egyptian minister of culture set up a commission of scientists, including aviation experts, to study the model plane. As a result of their report, it was made the centerpiece of an exhibition in the museum's main hall, where the model is now plainly labeled as a prototype aircraft.

Advanced technology

The report identified the model as a "cargo-carrying pusher-glider," a type that aeronautical designers are currently striving to perfect. Such an aircraft is intended to carry a vast payload, cheaply and at low speed, basically as a glider, but with a low-powered engine to provide forward thrust. Designers recognize that for this purpose it should have wings that curve downward at the tips. Like the modern Concorde on take-off and landing, it should also have a turned-down nose. These are all features of the Cairo model.

Legendary flight
According to Greek legend, the craftsman Daedalus and his son, Icarus, escaped imprisonment by soaring away from their captors on wings made of wax and feathers. But the wings worked too well and Icarus flew too close to the sun, causing his wax wings to melt and plunging him into the sea.

Ki-Kung-Shi's flying chariot
Chinese legend states that in about 1760 craftsman Ki-Kung-Shi built a flying chariot. The emperor ordered it to be destroyed because the art of flying was reserved for imperial use only.

The discovery of an ancient model of a flying device came as a shock to Western scientists, but Indian and Eastern scholars were not particularly surprised. The sacred histories of India, Tibet, and other cultures refer many times to the flying vehicles of early rulers and their use for transportation and warfare.

Indian texts give details of the metals and wood sheeting needed for the construction of flying machines. Called *vimanas*, they were not supported by wings but supposedly derived their levitation and thrust from natural forces in the earth and atmosphere. Disc-shaped and luminous, they sound somewhat like the stereotype of a modern UFO (unidentified flying object).

Ancient flight

It is only quite recently that Western scientists have started paying attention to their colleagues in Asia, who have always taken such accounts seriously. In 1928 Dr. Bertholt Laufer of the Field Columbian Museum, Chicago, made a positive assessment in his essay "The

---

The Nazca Indians may have discovered how to construct hot-air balloons; if so, they would have been able to observe their linear designs from above.

Prehistory of Aviation" of the records on ancient flight. On a more popular level, mystery writers such as Desmond Leslie have found and quoted many of the old records as background and support for UFO stories.

Sound and vision

A common feature in universal traditions of past flight is that it involved the use of sound. Tribal shamans in Africa, Siberia, and North America still practice trance flight, a reportedly controlled form of out-of-body experience. This, they claim, is a remnant of the more developed arts of their ancient predecessors, whose flights were performed physically. By means of a rhythmic beat the shaman's drum would apparently rise into the air, carrying the shaman along with it.

Some archeologists are suggesting that mysterious great works of prehistory, such as the system of lines and images spread across the Nazca plateau in Peru, which can only be appreciated from above, may have originally been viewed by means of shamanic flight. But it now seems probable that there is a more rational explanation that still involves viewing the lines from the air. The Nazca Indians may have discovered how to construct hot-air balloons; if so, they would have been able to observe their linear designs from above.

Aerial view
In November 1975 American Bill Spohrer and fellow members of the International Explorers' Society built a hot-air balloon. They employed only technology and materials that would have been available to the Nazca Indians at the time of the construction of the mysterious Nazca lines. Two men suspended in a reed gondola were able to view the lines as they flew over the desert.

CHAPTER SIX

LOST CIVILIZATIONS

Few ideas have captured the modern imagination more than the intriguing thought that a highly developed society may have preceded our own, and disappeared without trace thousands of years ago.

During a visit to Egypt in 590 B.C., the great Athenian lawgiver Solon had been discussing the history of humankind with the priests at the city of Sais. They smiled at his version of events. Solon then listened in wonder as the priests told their story.

"You Greeks are mere babes completely ignorant of the past. You know nothing of the rise and fall of the mighty empire of Atlantis and the part the city of Athens played in resisting its orgy of conquest."

They went on to describe how Atlantis, some 9,000 years before Solon's visit, had conquered the lands bordering the

Mediterranean Sea, only to be stopped by the heroic citizens of Athens. After this mighty struggle, the Atlantean homeland was suddenly overwhelmed by a cataclysmic disaster of fire and flood. The people of Atlantis, for their many crimes against humanity and their overweening pride, were swept from the stage of history by the outraged gods.

An epic story
This great drama allegedly impressed Solon so much that he vowed that on his return to Greece he would write an epic poem on the subject. The sources for this story are Plato's *Timaeus* and *Critias*, the two works the Greek philosopher probably wrote about 360 B.C. Plato claimed that he had heard the story from his cousin Critias the Younger who had heard it from his grandfather Critias. The elder Critias's father Dropides is said to have heard it from Solon himself. Critias was certain that Solon had told the truth and that he would have written his poem if he had not become involved in politics following his return from Egypt.

Fictional device?
One of the most widely used translations of Plato's works was by the distinguished 19th-century Greek scholar Benjamin Jowett. He thought that Plato's Atlantis was a fiction, a device that enabled Plato to advance his ideas concerning politics, social conditions, and the ideal society.

Many people have believed in Atlantis, and that its majestic rise to greatness and terrible fall must have happened. And many have attempted to show precisely where and when these events took place. This fascination with

The Greek lawgiver Solon

lost Atlantis, which in many cases amounted to an obsession with proving its existence, has produced a flood of ill-researched books, few of which have any real scientific support. Jowett himself wrote: "There is no kind or degree of absurdity or fancy in which the more foolish writers, both of antiquity and of modern times, have not indulged respecting it."

Atlantis has attracted, among others, explorers, historians, occultists, mystics, and novelists. And the lost continent of Atlantis has been located variously in the Atlantic Ocean, off the coast of Germany, Morocco, near the Bahamas, and southwest of Peru.

Identity problems
The description of Atlantis given by Plato appears to be implausible. Lying beyond the Straits of Gibraltar on islands in the Atlantic, it supposedly dominated Libya and Europe. But there is no geological evidence that such islands ever existed.

In addition, the war with the Athenians and the great catastrophe of fire and flood is supposed to have taken place 9,000 years before Solon's visit to Egypt. However, Plato's description of the great bustling metropolis of Atlantis frequently mentions gold, copper, and tin. But not iron. This would indicate a Bronze Age culture, which occurred much later in Greece, from about 2500 B.C. to 1200 B.C.

More problems arise if the destruction of Atlantis was really about 9600 B.C. At that time northern Europe was still suffering from the effects of the last Ice Age. Even the Mediterranean could not have supported the pleasant life-style Plato attributes to the Atlanteans.

Spectacular descriptions
According to Plato, Critias described not only the greatness of the Atlantean empire, the many things brought to their island in trade and tribute from foreign countries, the landscape, the woods, the rich fruits and vegetables; but he also described the spectacular architecture and fortifications of their marvelously

Ritual origins
Cretan bull baiters in a painting by English artist John Duncan. The picture follows the style of Minoan artists, and the colors and the border are the same as those used by native craftsmen. Plato mentions Atlantean rituals involving bulls that sound similar to those of Minoan Crete.

decorated metropolis. The Atlanteans' powerful navy of galleys was catered for by efficient, well-equipped ports, the largest of which was packed with vessels and merchants from overseas. Religious rituals were described, which included the hunting and slaying of a wild bull.

However, the saying of the first century A.D. Roman historian Tacitus that all power corrupts, and absolute power corrupts absolutely, seems to have undoubtedly applied to the Atlanteans. According to Plato they became "tainted with unrighteous ambition and power." They embarked on a dreadful war of aggression and were finally destroyed by fire and flood.

Human tragedy

Was this story of human tragedy a total fiction? Benjamin Jowett thought so. But he wrote in 1892, before the eminent English archeologist Sir Arthur Evans first began his excavations of the Palace of Minos at Knossos in Crete in 1900.

As early as 1909 it was suggested by K. T. Frost in an article in *The Times* of

> ## "Plato's words describe the scenes on the Vapheio cups which represent catching wild bulls for the Minoan bullfight."
>
> ### K. T. Frost

London that Plato's Atlantis was based on a genuine Egyptian tradition of Minoan Crete. Frost pointed out the correspondences between the island of Crete, its position with respect to the other islands in the eastern Mediterranean, and relevant descriptions by Plato. The correspondence between the ruling systems in Minoan Crete and Atlantis was noted.

"The great harbour...its shipping and its merchants coming from all parts, the elaborate bathrooms, the stadium, and the solemn sacrifice of a bull are all thoroughly, though not exclusively, Minoan; but when we read how the bull is hunted 'in the Temple of

Poseidon without weapons but with staves and nooses' we have an unmistakable description of the bullring at Knossos, the very thing that struck foreigners most and which gave rise to the legend of the Minotaur. Plato's words describe exactly the scenes on the

famous Vapheio cups which certainly represent catching wild bulls for the Minoan bullfight."

Minoan nobles wore purple robes, colored using dye from the murex, a type of whelk. Similarly Plato's Atlantean kings, after sacrificing the bull, "put on beautiful azure robes and, sitting on the ground at night, over the embers of the sacrifices by which they had sworn...they received and gave judgment."

Volcanic destruction

In about 1450 B.C. the Minoans, like the Atlanteans, perished in fire and flood. Prof. Spyridon Marinatos, director general of Greek antiquities, published an article in 1939 entitled "The Volcanic Destruction of Minoan Crete." His conclusions were inspired by his archeological study of a villa in the Minoan port of Amnisos.

Raging bull
This cup is one of a pair found in 1889 in a tomb near Vapheio, Laconia, Greece. It shows bull hunting, and is thought to have been made in Crete in the late 16th century B.C.

POSEIDON'S SONS
According to legend, the islands of Atlantis represent the share of the world allocated to the god Poseidon. The islands were ruled by his five pairs of sons, so Atlantis was divided into ten parts. Two springs, one of warm water, the other of cold, flowed from the earth, and every variety of food grew in great profusion from the soil. Circular, concentric channels were built enclosing the central mountain, through which channels the sea flowed. The descendants of Atlas, Poseidon's eldest son, and his brothers, inherited this island paradise generation after generation.

Ring of water
A modern painting of the city of Atlantis, based on Plato's account, showing the channels of sea water that supposedly enclosed a central mountain.

PSYCHIC NEWS FROM ATLANTIS

The only original descriptions we have of Atlantis come from two texts by the Greek philosopher Plato in his **Dialogues** *of c. 350 B.C. However, many writers have provided a wealth of additional "psychic" knowledge about the "lost continent."*

MOST PSYCHICS WHO have allegedly supplied information about the lost continent of Atlantis claim either to be in touch with long-dead Atlanteans or report clairvoyant visions or memories of their own former lives on Atlantis. However, few of these accounts are consistent with one another. One of the earliest visionaries was the Austrian Rudolph Steiner (1861–1925), who claimed to have psychic access to the so-called Akashic Records, a kind of cosmic library in which the entire history of the universe is stored. Steiner reported that the Atlanteans had enormous powers of memory, could control the "life force" and extract it from plants, and rode in powered vehicles that floated above the ground.

Daphne Vigers, in contrast, in *Atlantis Rising* (1944), gathered her knowledge of Atlantis from "astral experiences," in which she claimed she saw the continent's "common-sense economy and an efficient system of public utilities" – and also its sun-worshiping high priest.

Murray Hope, in *Atlantis — Myth or Reality?* (1991), describes his "far memories" of an Atlantis that practiced "a form of socialism" under some sort of divine guidance. Hope claimed that "the Atlanteans' main source of energy was sonics," whose secret was closely guarded by priest-scientists. The people were tall, either fair or copper-skinned, with slanted eyes.

Crystal power

American healer Edgar Cayce (1877–1945) – whose least extraordinary claim concerning his previous incarnations was to have been an Atlantean – followed Rudolph Steiner in believing he had tapped into the Akashic Records. From them he learned, he said, that the Atlanteans used crystals as a power source. Like many other psychics, he attributed the fall of Atlantis not to a natural disaster but to abuse of power – both spiritual and material – by the ruling caste, which led to a cataclysmic nuclear disaster about 10,000 B.C. But Cayce also felt able to predict when Atlantis would rise again: In 1940 he rashly announced that the sunken continent would emerge from the sea in the Bahamas in 1968 or 1969.

Finding that the displacement of great blocks of stone could not be attributed to an earthquake but might well be the result of tidal waves carrying the blocks away in their backwash, Prof. Marinatos rethought the question of the destruction of Minoan Crete. He wrote: "...there is little reason to doubt that the devastation of the coast sites of Minoan Crete was caused by the waves from the eruptions of Thera." Subsequently in 1950 he wrote: "The Egyptians must have learnt of an island being submerged and this was Thera, but being so small and insignificant they did not know of it. They transferred this event to Crete, the island so grievously struck and with which they suddenly lost all contact."

Prof. Marinatos was more and more convinced that the island of Thera (now known as Santorini) was the location of Plato's Atlantis. He saw his discovery in 1967 of a Minoan settlement buried at Akrotiri on Thera as climactic confirmation of the theory he had held so long.

Another academic, the volcanologist Prof. A. G. Galanopoulos likewise became convinced of the basic truth of Plato's Atlantis story. From 1957 he outlined his main hypothesis, giving a wealth of supporting evidence. As a seismologist he accepted that the shock waves, volcanic fall-out, and tidal waves caused by the eruption on the island of Thera about 1450 B.C. caused the utter destruction of the Minoan empire.

Cataclysmic collapse

Prof. Galanopoulos went even further. He considered Thera in its pre-eruption state to have been as important to the Minoans as Crete itself. Pointing out that Plato's description of the Atlantean metropolis was reminiscent of a small volcanic island, he showed how closely pre-eruption Thera fitted this account. Perhaps, he argued, there were two islands, with Crete in the role of Plato's "royal state," and Thera cast as the "metropolis," the center of Minoan life. The cataclysm at Thera, leading to the final collapse of the central 32 square

The past revealed
The archeological site at Akrotiri on the island of Santorini, where the Greek archeologist Prof. Spyridon Marinatos uncovered a Minoan settlement.

miles of island into the abyss at the center of the volcano, would have destroyed the most densely populated areas, sweeping away palaces, mansions and other Atlantean edifices, leaving only those settlements that existed on the periphery of the island to be excavated from their shroud of pumice by the archeologists over 3,000 years later.

One of Prof. Galanopoulos's most intriguing arguments deals with the question of the dimensions of Plato's Atlantis and of the date given for its existence and destruction. According to Critias, Solon was led to believe that it all took place 9,000 years before his visit to Egypt. In addition the great plain of Atlantis is said to have covered an area of 994 by 685 miles. Atlantis maintained a huge army of over 1,000,000 men, and so on, all impossibly large figures in the light of what we know of Minoan Crete.

> ## The cataclysm at Thera would have destroyed the most densely populated areas, sweeping away palaces, mansions and other Atlantean edifices.

Prof. Galanopoulos suggested that an error of a factor of 10 had been made in all large numbers over 1,000 so that the true dimensions of length and time, numbers of men, and so on, are obtained by dividing every figure given by 10. If this adjustment is made, the interval of time before Solon's visit to the Egyptian priests in 590 B.C. becomes 900 years instead

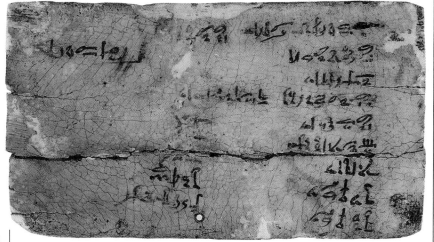

of 9,000. Adding 900 to 590 B.C. gives 1490 B.C., which must be close to the fatal date when Thera erupted. The size of the great plain of Atlantis becomes 99 by 68 miles, a much more reasonable area and approximately the size of Crete's plain of Messara. An army of 100,000 men is still large but not impossibly so. The numbers below 1,000 are unchanged, so that the length of the canal from the metropolis center to the sea remains 5 miles, giving the diameter of the metropolis as 11 miles, a figure that Prof. Galanopoulos intriguingly points out must have been close to the original diameter of Thera before it erupted and collapsed.

Accurate account?
Is an error of this kind possible? It may be. If Prof. Galanopoulos's theory is accepted, Plato's account of the fabulous kingdom of Atlantis and its terrible fate then becomes a remarkably faithful account of the life and death of the Minoans, the first great European civilization. And thus what Solon heard from the Egyptian priests of Sais was probably based on the archival accounts of the great disaster that were told to their predecessors almost a thousand years before by Minoan refugees fleeing from the wreckage of their island. Little did they know that their lost homeland would give rise to the legend of Atlantis, and that it would fascinate generations through the centuries to come.

Ancient decoration
A section of a fresco from the wall of a Minoan house, dating from the 16th century B.C., which was discovered at an archeological site at Akrotiri on the island of Santorini.

Early translation
This writing board comes from Egypt's 18th Dynasty (1567–1320 B.C.) and is headed "How to make names of Keftiu [Minoan]." Egyptian schoolboys used such boards to write out Cretan names and their Egyptian equivalents in parallel columns.

LANGUAGE PROBLEMS
Errors may have been introduced into ancient records concerning Atlantis in the course of their translation from the Minoan language into Egyptian, and then into Greek. As Critias, Plato's cousin, explained to his friends:

"I ought to warn you that you must not be surprised if you should perhaps hear Hellenic names given to foreigners. I will tell you the reason for this: Solon, who was intending to use the tale for his poem, inquired into the meaning of the names, and found that the early Egyptians in writing them down had translated them into their own language, and he recovered the meaning of the several names and when copying them out again translated them into our language. My grandfather had the original writing, which is still in my possession, and was carefully studied by me when I was a child."

DREAMS OF LEMURIA

There are some accounts of Atlantis that describe it as a real, physical island continent in the middle of the Atlantic Ocean, which also refer to another intriguing lost continent — Lemuria.

ANY "OCCULTIST" COMMENTATORS believe that the inhabitants of Lemuria were highly developed long before Atlantis reached its glory — and, indeed, that the latter was originally a colony of Lemuria. Perhaps most surprising of all, they can cite eminent 19th-century scientists who firmly believed that such a continent had to exist.

The occult history of Lemuria begins with the founder of a new spiritual system called Theosophy, Madame Helena Petrovna Blavatsky (1831–91). Madame Blavatsky was nothing if not colorful — she was at various times a bareback rider in a circus, a "psychic" whose spiritualist society was closed amid charges of fraud, and an intrepid traveler. She emerged in due course, in her supporters' eyes, as one of the most profound and original spiritual thinkers in history.

The "root races"

In Madame Blavatsky's cosmology, propounded in her monumental and frequently obscure *The Secret Doctrine* (1886), humanity has evolved (and still is evolving) through a series of seven "root races." The first, invisible creatures of "fire mist," inhabited an "imperishable sacred land." The second, barely visible, lived in the "Arctic continent" of Hyperborea, and the Lemurians were the third. The fourth root race were the Atlanteans, and present-day humanity is the fifth. From us the sixth will evolve to live on Lemuria once again. The seventh will depart from Earth and live on Mercury.

According to Madame Blavatsky's highly controversial and totally unsupported worldview, Lemuria occupied most of the Southern Hemisphere "from the foot of the Himalayas to within a few degrees of the Antarctic Circle." A volcanic cataclysm apparently destroyed the continent more than 40 million years ago. In Blavatsky's and later Theosophists' accounts, the Lemurians were not the civilized beings that some later writers have claimed

Influential spiritualist
Madame Blavatsky convinced her Theosophical supporters of the existence of Lemuria.

them to be. They were 15-foot-tall, ape-like, egg-laying hermaphrodites who lived in holes in the ground and communicated telepathically. Although they lacked proper brains, their willpower could literally move mountains. Some had four arms; some had an eye in the back of the head for "psychic vision." They had protruding muzzles, but otherwise flat faces, with eyes set far apart, thus enabling them to see sideways. Their strangest feature was their feet, which had a protruding heel that let them walk backward as easily as forward.

Elusive wisdom

Madame Blavatsky claimed to have received her information from a sacred book of ancient wisdom kept secretly in Tibet. Called the *Book of Dyzan,* it was written on palm leaves in the lost Atlantean language of Senzar. Its contents were reportedly revealed to her during "astral visits" from the ethereal "Brotherhood of Mahatmas" who, she argued, direct human affairs from their mountain hideaway on the Roof of the World. Madame Blavatsky's successors, who elaborated on the details of Lemurian life, history, and geography, claimed that they had gained their information from "astral clairvoyance" or "occult revelations from the

> **Madame Blavatsky claimed to have received her information about Lemuria from a book of ancient wisdom kept in Tibet. Called the *Book of Dyzan*, it was written on palm leaves in the lost Atlantean language of Senzar.**

Theosophical Masters." But the Theosophists did have several respectable sources for their belief that there had once been a Lemurian continent. For the concept of Lemuria at least had its origins in a thoroughly logical scientific debate.

Evolutionary discrepancy

When Charles Darwin published his *Origin of Species* in 1859, his theory of evolution did not convince everyone. Many opposed it, as they do today, on religious grounds. Darwin postulated that each species evolved over millions of years from a common ancestor. But there was a problem: The theory, if true, meant that the species of mammals we know today should be limited to their own particular territories — unlike birds, which can and do migrate from one landmass to another. Specifically, there was a mystery as to how the lemur, a small mammal related to both humans and monkeys, managed to appear both on the island of Madagascar

THE MYTH OF MU

"With thunderous roarings the doomed land sank. Down, down, down she went, into the mouth of hell."

ATLANTIS MAY REPRESENT a legendary memory of a real, vanished culture, but the myth of the lost continent of Mu has never been more than a fantasy. Those believers who claimed that it actually existed could not even agree on its location.

The most notorious modern proponent of the Mu legend was the Anglo-American former Bengal Lancer Col. James Churchward, who in *The Lost Continent of Mu* (1926) maintained that he had translated a secret collection of sacred scripts that he had found in India (or in Tibet, according to his later writings).

These scripts apparently described the earth's creation and the emergence of humankind: "the Garden of Eden was not in Asia but on a now sunken continent in the Pacific Ocean. The biblical story of creation — the epic of the seven days and seven nights — came first not from the peoples of the Nile or of the Euphrates Valley but from this now submerged continent, Mu — the Motherland of Man."

According to Churchward all this took place 200,000 years ago on an island continent that stretched 6,000 miles from what are now the Marianas in the western Pacific to Easter Island in the east, and 3,000 miles from Hawaii in the north to Mangaia in the south. Churchward made the fantastic claim that the Pacific islands are the last visible remnants of this huge continent.

Churchward also claimed that he had translated a collection of tablets found in Mexico by American engineer William Niven. Churchward managed this feat by what he considered to be an occult technique — staring at the symbols until their meaning rose into his mind from his "inner consciousness." The tablets, Churchward's mystical insight informed him, were not Aztec as scholars thought, but had been written "more than 12,000 years ago....All but a few of them are picture writings, and are tableaus depicting sentences from the Sacred Inspired Writings of Mu."

A handsome people

Churchward undertook further research in India and established at least to his own satisfaction that Mu was a highly sophisticated and civilized society, consisting of 64 million people living in 10 tribes under a single government. The dominant race was "a white race, exceedingly handsome people, with clear white or olive skins, large, soft, dark eyes, and straight black hair. Besides this white race, there were other races, people with yellow, brown, or black skins."

Churchward believed that the Muvians, as he called this race, were unsurpassed engineers and architects, superb navigators who colonized many distant lands (including Atlantis), and extremely affluent, thanks to the richness of their soil and their highly-developed skill at agriculture and industry. But this peace-loving "center of the earth's civilization" was, Churchward said, abruptly destroyed in a cataclysmic upheaval 12,000 years ago: "With thunderous roarings the doomed land sank. Down, down, down she went, into the mouth of hell."

Churchward was not the first to describe Mu nor the first to apply more imagination than scholarship to his material. Most people now regard his books about Mu as an early, romantic form of science fiction.

and in other countries around the Indian Ocean. Darwin's opponents took great pleasure in discovering this flaw in his theory, and pointed out that it proved their own thesis: that the variety of life was the handiwork of God, and that He had distributed animals about the globe according to His own divine preference.

The pro-evolutionist biologists rapidly countered with a hypothesis of their own, and one that did not conflict with Darwin's theory. They reasoned that when the mammals were still evolving

> The hypothetical lost continent neatly solved the so-called "missing link," the elusive fossil evidence of intermediate species between the apes and man.

into their present forms, there had been a vast landmass connecting the lemur's various present habitats. This landmass was dubbed Lemuria by the English zoologist Philip L. Sclater.

To conform with this hypothesis, Lemuria would have had to have been truly vast. The eminent 19th-century naturalist A. R. Wallace calculated that "If...it comprised the whole area now inhabited by Lemuroid animals, we must make it extend from West Africa to Burma, South China and Celebes."

Primeval home
Ernst H. Haeckel, a German biologist, took the argument further, to explain the distribution of Homo sapiens around the globe. There were, he wrote, "a number of circumstances ...[that] suggest that the primeval home of man was a continent now sunk beneath the surface of the Indian Ocean, which extended along the south of Asia, as it is at present (and probably in direct connection with it)...as far as Further India and the Sunda Islands [and] west as far

as Madagascar and the southeastern shores of Africa." The existence of an enormous lost continent would, said Haeckel, "greatly facilitate the explanation of the geographical distribution of the human species by migration."

The "missing link"
The hypothetical lost continent neatly solved another of Darwin's difficulties: the so-called "missing link," the elusive fossil evidence of intermediate species between the apes and man. The fossil links were missing because they had sunk with the landmass of Lemuria.

In the hands of the Theosophists the continent of Lemuria, its role in the evolution of humankind, and its cataclysmic disappearance were transformed from a reasonable scientific proposition into an unbelievable scenario that had no logical justification.

Scientists have long since discarded the Lemurian hypothesis. The theories of continental drift and tectonic plates help to explain the distribution of species, as the modern continents split away from an original single landmass. The same theories also diminish hope that any of the "sunken lost continents" ever had any basis in geological reality.

Ernst H. Haeckel
Biologist Ernst Haeckel believed that there was a long-lost continent lying beneath the Indian Ocean.

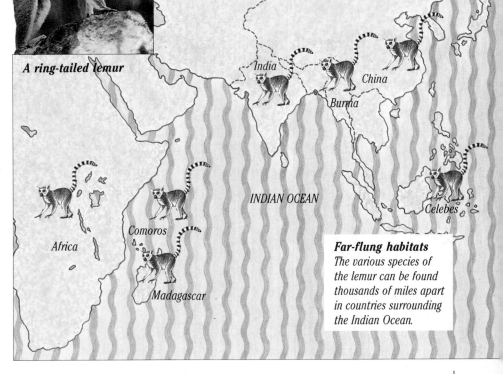

A ring-tailed lemur

India

China

Burma

INDIAN OCEAN

Celebes

Africa

Comoros

Madagascar

Far-flung habitats
The various species of the lemur can be found thousands of miles apart in countries surrounding the Indian Ocean.

QUESTS FOR A GOLDEN CITY

The lure of riches, of wealth beyond the dreams of avarice, has inspired some strange quests in history, and has cost the life of many a fortune-hunter.

So GREAT IS THE DESIRE for treasure that many have set out on the most perilous expeditions with little more to guide them than rumor and hearsay. Tales of a very different kind have driven others to seek long-lost or hidden centers of spiritual riches. In both cases, some travelers have returned from their quests with all that they sought. More often, these adventurers have returned empty-handed — albeit, in some cases, the wiser for their experience.

One of the most common rumors to capture the imagination of medieval Europeans appears to have started life in 1145, at a meeting near Rome between Bishop Otto of Freising, Bavaria, and Bishop Hugh of Gebal (now Jubayl in Lebanon). Bishop Hugh allegedly recounted that he had heard tell of a wise and mighty Christian ruler, whose empire — of fabulous wealth and splendor — lay far beyond the river Tigris (in modern-day Iraq), and even beyond Persia.

Christianity besieged

The priest-emperor's name was Presbyter Johannes (meaning "John the Priest"), and he became known as Prester John. He was said to be anxious to assist the forces of Christendom. This was music to the bishops' ears, for at that time the Church felt besieged both militarily and spiritually by the forces of Islam (in the form of the Saracens), who were threatening Jerusalem. To oust them, King Louis VII of France was preparing the Second Crusade.

Prester John, according to Bishop Hugh's information, had already attempted to aid the European Christians but had been unable to cross the river Tigris with his army. This hitherto unheard-of ally was still more attractive to the elders of the Christian Church for another reason: Prester John was allegedly a direct descendant of one of the Magi, the Three Wise Men who were led by a heavenly sign to visit the new-born Jesus Christ in Bethlehem.

So dazzled by this account was the Christian community that in September 1177 — three years before the Third Crusade set out in an attempt to try to right the disastrous failure of the Second — Pope Alexander III sent an emissary (his own physician) into the

Elusive realm
In this 16th-century map of Africa the position of Prester John's elusive realm is represented by the upside-down figure in the center.

Godly connection
"Adoration of the Magi," by German artist Hans Memling (c. 1430–94). The mysterious Prester John was supposed to be a direct descendant of one of the Three Wise Men.

uncharted East with a letter to Prester John. The doctor was never seen again, but the conviction that the mysterious Christian empire in the East existed did not wane. Even Moses Maimonides (1135–1204), one of the great sages of Judaism, referred in his writings to Prester John's empire as an established fact.

In the early 1240's, more "evidence" emerged, in the form of a letter purportedly written in Arabic by John himself to the emperor of Constantinople in 1165. In it, John identified his realm as "the three Indies," and

Crusading Christians
A 14th-century illumination showing crusaders on their way into battle.

explorer Marco Polo, early in the 14th century) that John himself had either died at the hands of the warlord Genghis Khan or been forced to become his vassal.

Traveler's tales

In the 1320's, the Dominican friar Jordanus de Sévérac traveled through India and was told that Prester John now lived in the rump of his empire in Ethiopia. This fitted with the known fact that the Ethiopians were Christians, and by the curious synchronicity that attended each resurgence of the Prester John legend, exactly suited the political needs of Europe. The problem was how to make contact with such a potentially invaluable ally,

---

As European travelers eventually penetrated into Asia — and found no trace there of either a Christian king or a great empire — the belief in Prester John persisted but the location of his realm subtly changed.

---

whose forces could open a second front against the armies of Islam. Almost a century later, the continuing lure of Prester John remained strong enough to intrigue King Henry the Navigator of Portugal. He, and from 1460, his successor King João II, both made attempts to contact John in his mountain kingdom, but failed. One of their messengers, Pero da Covilham, actually managed to reach the Ethiopian court of King Alexander in 1494, but it appears that he was subsequently refused permission to leave by Alexander's successor — and died there years later, having been given a wife and land by his captors.

Two more Portuguese emissaries managed to reach Ethiopia some time before 1512, and on receiving word from them in 1514, King Emmanuel sent a further party of ambassadors to join them. After a journey of almost six years, the group arrived at "Prester John's palace" — a tent in the Abyssinian interior. The "emperor" within was a nomad chieftain named Lebna Dengel Dawit, who, although undoubtedly rich and certainly Christian, was hardly the splendid and powerful priest-king of the legend of Prester John.

among other extravagances (including hares as big as sheep and men with four eyes) he claimed to receive tribute from no less than 72 kings, among them the leaders of the 10 Lost Tribes of Israel.

Journeys into Asia

Belief in the existence of Prester John's empire was as much an act of faith as a product of political and military wishful thinking. Only this can possibly explain two notable facts: first, that as European travelers eventually penetrated into Asia — and found no trace there of either a Christian king or a great empire — the belief in Prester John persisted but the location of his realm subtly changed. And second that Prester John did not seem to age as the centuries passed. The belief remained despite reports (one, for instance, from the

Henry the Navigator

131

And, after 1527, when the diplomatic mission finally arrived in Lisbon once again and described what they had found, the Prester John myth inevitably began to crumble. The political and religious shape of Europe had already begun to change by then: The threat posed by Islam had receded, and the fabulous riches of the New World beckoned. The Prester John legend had lasted nearly 400 years, but only endured as long as it was needed.

Source of rumor

Was there ever a real Prester John? There are some scholars who believe that Lebna Dengel Dawit was the descendant of the legendary king. However, the famous letter dated 1165 is almost certainly a 13th-century fabrication. There were Christian kings in Asia, but it seems likely that the ruler from beyond Persia who inspired the original rumor was not a Christian at all, but the Mongolian warlord Genghis Khan. His reputation became confused with tales of distant Christian kingdoms and was transformed by Chinese whispers, time, and distance, into a figure that answered a profound psychological and emotional longing.

Warrior archetype
The legendary Mongolian warlord Genghis Khan (c. 1162–1227) was one of the world's most notorious conquerors. It is possible that stories about Khan may have provided the basis for the character of Prester John.

The Indians habitually wore gold and emeralds and even decorated the outsides of their houses with gold.

If Prester John's empire appealed to both spiritual and material needs, the hunt for some legendary golden cities has been as a result of sheer greed. One such was El Dorado, rumors of which first reached European ears when the first governor of Venezuela, Ambrosius Dalfinger, arrived on the shores of Lake Maracaibo in September 1529. Here he found the local people festooned with gold ornaments, and was told that the precious metal came from a people in the country's highlands, "where the salt comes from." They were so rich that their king — El Dorado, the "gilded one" — was said to have been painted gold permanently. Dalfinger's own attempt to find this fabulous treasure house ended in disaster, as did an expedition mounted by his successor, Georg Hohermuth, in 1535.

Golden ritual

But in June 1536, Gonzalo Jimenez de Queseda, a Spanish lawyer turned adventurer, found the "place of gold" — the Chibcha Indian village of Hunsa, over 9,000 feet up in the mountains of what is now Colombia. The inhabitants had amassed their wealth by trading in salt. They habitually wore gold and emeralds and even decorated the outsides of their houses with gold, while their chief sat resplendent in a throne room lined with thick gold sheets, surrounded by gold plate and yet more emeralds. The story of the "golden man" turned out to be accurate, too, for at his coronation the Chibcha king was ritually covered in gum and then coated with gold dust. This "golden man" was then immersed in Lake Guatavita until the gold was washed off, as an offering to the gods.

Queseda helped himself to all the gold he and his men could carry. Despite the phenomenal wealth he stole on that occasion, he remained convinced to the end of his life that he had failed to find the real El Dorado. Queseda made two further expeditions, both unsuccessful, before he died in 1579.

Golden armor
A 500-year-old gold chest piece from South America.

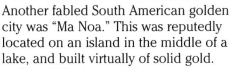

Chibcha Indian tradition has it that each new king was coated in gold and taken to the center of the lake on a raft. He would then be immersed in the waters, while large amounts of gold and jewels were tipped overboard. Since the middle of the 16th century treasure hunters have searched without success for the lake's hidden hoards.

Another fabled South American golden city was "Ma Noa." This was reputedly located on an island in the middle of a lake, and built virtually of solid gold.

One of the latest and strangest quests to find Ma Noa was undertaken by Col. Percy H. Fawcett, an artillery officer in the British Indian Army who was born in 1867. Fawcett's interest in the golden city appeared to stem from his belief, based on an 18th-century document he had found in Rio de Janeiro, that "amazing ruins of ancient cities — ruins incomparably older than those of Egypt — exist in the far interior of the Mato Grosso."

Futile search

This region of central Brazil is still the world's largest unexplored area, and, whether in the hope of finding tons of gold or a place in the annals of archeology, Fawcett began his brave adventure from Cuyaba, in the Mato Grosso jungle region, in the spring of 1925. He reported his position on May 30, and was never heard of again. For the next quarter of a century Fawcett was variously reported to have been seen alive, or to have been killed, in different circumstances, and in many places over an area of perhaps a quarter of a million square miles. His actual fate remains as mysterious as the reality of the "lost cities" he set out to find.

Mining mystery

The lust for gold, no less single-minded than the one that drove the Spanish conquistadors in South America, fueled the belief that Great Zimbabwe in southern Africa was the site of the fabled mines of King Solomon. According to the biblical account (1 Kings 10:14) Solomon's annual income in gold from the mines at Ophir and Tarshish was 666 talents, or about 700,000 ounces — today worth the sum of US$230 million. Of this, some 420 talents came from the mine at Ophir. Like many other places named in the Old Testament, the exact locations of Ophir and Tarshish are today something of an enigma. But in the 16th century, as the Portuguese drove the Arab traders from the coasts of what is now Mozambique, the Arabs told alluring

> "Amazing ruins of ancient cities — ruins incomparably older than those of Egypt — exist in the far interior of the Mato Grosso."
>
> **Col. Percy H. Fawcett**

Col. Percy H. Fawcett
The intrepid explorer disappeared on a quest for ancient, undiscovered cities in the Mato Grosso jungles of Brazil in 1925.

♦ PAGE 135

WHERE WAS EDEN?

According to Genesis, God took six days to make the heavens and the earth. He then rested for a day before making Adam, the first man, "of dust from the ground." And then God created Eden.

"THE LORD GOD PLANTED a garden in Eden, in the east....A river flowed out of Eden to water the garden, and there it divided, and became four rivers. The name of the first is Pishon: it is the one which flows around the whole land of Havilah, where there is gold....The name of the second river is Gihon; it is the one which flows around the whole land of Cush. And the name of the third river is Tigris, which flows east of Assyria. And the fourth river is the Euphrates" (Genesis 2:10–14).

This is the closest the biblical account comes to pinpointing a geographical location for the paradise in which Adam and Eve lived before being expelled for eating the fruit of the tree of knowledge of good and evil. And, ever since that time, wise men and scholars have speculated on where, precisely, the Garden of Eden may have been located.

Possible locations

The description is far from exact. The Tigris does not have a common head with the Euphrates, and the Pishon and Gihon have never been satisfactorily identified. Scholars have put forward the theory that Pishon might represent the Persian Gulf and Gihon the Nile, and so Mesopotamia and Armenia have been cited as possible locations.

The Garden of Paradise found?
Although the Tigris and Euphrates rivers do not share a common head, their tributaries meet at Al Qurna in southern Iraq. This has long been considered a possible site for the Garden of Eden.

> ## "Like all true places, it [Eden] is not on any map."
> ### Joseph Conrad

During the Middle Ages some churchmen believed that Eden had escaped the devastation of the Flood because it was on a mountaintop. Some thought it might have been an island, while others hypothesized that it could lie within the borders of Prester John's elusive realm.

Furthermore, it has been suggested that the Garden of Eden was in Syria — that is, "eastward" of Judea, the place where the Book of Genesis is believed to have been written — or even in Jerusalem itself, for that was where Jesus Christ redeemed the "sin" of Adam, and it seemed logical and fitting that he should do so in the very place from which Adam was evicted.

The intrepid explorers of the great age of discovery in the 15th and 16th centuries incorporated the search for a physical Eden into their travels into the unknown. None had any success. Curiously enough, the most famous of them all, Christopher Columbus (1451–1506), came to see Eden as a metaphysical entity, and concluded that Eden was a place "whither no one might go but by God's permission." This might explain the biblical location of Eden in a golden "somewhere" just outside any place to be found in the known world.

An artistic view
This painting of "Adam and Eve in Paradise" by Jan Brueghel (1568–1625) and Peter Paul Rubens (1577–1640) provides a traditional interpretation of the Garden of Eden. Brueghel painted the landscape, the flowers, and the animals, and Rubens painted the figures.

tales of a vast inland empire whose ruler lived in a palace plated with gold. The capital, built near the mines from which this gold was dug, they variously called Symbaoe, Zimbaoche, or Zunbanhy. There is little doubt that this was, in fact, Great Zimbabwe. Long before exploring the African interior, the Portuguese added some assumptions of their own to these stories, which only increased their appeal to the greed of the colonists.

Imaginative speculation

Based on reports he had received from Swahili traders, João de Barros wrote of Zimbabwe in 1552: "...as these edifices are very similar to some which are found in the land of Prester John at a place called Acaxumo, which was a municipal city of the Queen of Sheba... it would seem that the...lord of that state also owned these mines and therefore ordered these edifices to be raised there...."

The idea caught the imagination, and by 1609 the missionary João dos Santos was confidently proclaiming that Great Zimbabwe was none other than the biblical Ophir. The Portuguese never penetrated as far as Great Zimbabwe, but this speculation was considered to be factual for several hundred years.

Biblical connection

In 1871, an eccentric German explorer named Karl Mauch was led by a German-American ivory hunter named Adam Renders to Great Zimbabwe, which had until that time lain undiscovered by white men.

Legendary treasure
A stone figure found at
Great Zimbabwe. Treasure
hunters were convinced
that this was the site of
King Solomon's mines.

Several years after Mauch's expedition, he published a book in Germany in which he sought to resurrect the Ophir-Zimbabwe theory, and even asserted that the Queen of Sheba had maintained a palace there. Nothing could have helped open up southern Africa faster, as the lust for gold brought a flood of fortune hunters to the site. At one point in the 1890's a company was specially formed to plunder the ruins. It did indeed find a few ounces of gold at the site before the operation was shut down in the wake of archeologists' protests.

Exorcizing ghosts

In the late 19th and early 20th centuries the generally racist attitude of most archeologists and explorers was responsible for the belief that native Africans were not capable of constructing Great Zimbabwe. It was not until the advent of radiocarbon dating techniques that the ghost of King Solomon was finally exorcized from its stones. Research has now shown that this great complex was built in stages between about A.D. 1000 and 1425. There had been gold mines nearby, but far later than the reign of Solomon, who had lived about 950 B.C. The whereabouts of King Solomon's mines at Ophir and Tarshish still remain a mystery, although sites located as far apart as Mexico, Brazil, the Negev Desert, and India have been proposed.

Happily, not all quests for rich and mysteriously elusive cities have been fired by greed. The hunt for Prester John's empire was at least partly inspired by religious fervor. But two centers of supreme spiritual importance have captured the imagination

Great Zimbabwe
This complex of buildings, spread over a 60-acre site, was the center of the powerful and wealthy empire of the Shona people in the 14th and 15th centuries.

> By 1609 the missionary João dos Santos was confidently proclaiming that Great Zimbabwe was none other than the biblical Ophir.

ROUTE TO ECSTASY

French explorer Alexandra David-Neel called the secret land of Shambala "the Holy Place where the earthly world links with the highest states of consciousness."

The English writer Geoffrey Ashe, in his book *Atlantis, Lost Lands, Ancient Wisdom* (1992), outlines the path to Shambhala: "A Tibetan abbot describes the route [to Shambhala] after a fashion....However, no one can simply go there, even with the aid of the abbot's itinerary. A would-be pilgrim has first to be called. If he tries without being called, he perishes. Given enough holiness or mental powers, the route can be short-circuited. One Tashi Lama was transported there in an ecstasy."

of seekers of truth. One is the mysterious, hidden paradise of Shambhala, that has been described as "a northern place of quietude," which is said to be tucked into a concealed but immensely fertile valley somewhere in northern Tibet. Here, it is said, untroubled by the outside world, dwells a community of holy men.

Very many Asian traditions, ranging from Russia to China, also speak of such a peaceful place, and under many different names. But every one nestles safely in a secret valley, protected by the encircling mountains. And each of these peaceful places is on the border, or just beyond, the country most familiar to those who believe in its existence. Perhaps such a place did exist. Perhaps it still does. But it seems that the *belief* in such a place is more important than its physical reality.

Magical castle

Legend states that Camelot was the castle of Britain's most famous king, Arthur, son of Uther Pendragon. King Arthur has never been satisfactorily identified with any known, named historical figure, but so powerful is the Arthurian myth that to have taken root so strongly it may well have grown from some actual historical core. King Arthur might have been an unusually powerful warlord of fifth-century A.D., post-Roman, southwestern Britain. The magical castle of Camelot described in the medieval Arthurian romances may well not exist, if only because a "castle" in the fifth century was a very different thing from the castles known to the

"King Arthur and the Thirty Kingdoms"
An illustration from the English canon Peter Longtoft's 13th-century history of England.

poets and epic prose writers who, nearly 1,000 years later, chronicled the brave deeds of the legendary King Arthur and his courageous knights.

The Camelot of literature is both a magic and an ideal place. It is specifically not Arthur's capital, but purely his castle, his headquarters. And no one reigns at Camelot before or after him. But it is also from Camelot that the noble knights of the Round Table ride forth to show the world the true meaning of chivalry, and it is also from Camelot that Arthur instigates his knights' mystic quest to discover the Holy Grail.

As English writer and expert on the Arthurian legend, Geoffrey Ashe notes in his book *The Mythology of the British Isles* (1990), in Camelot "we confront a medieval dream-city which it would be misguided to locate on any map." Elsewhere, Ashe writes that "the Camelot of romance has lost touch with history and geography. It is a symbol, conjuring up a golden age in chivalric terms."

It is clearly fruitless to identify such a place with any historic settlement, although the list of candidates proposed down the centuries is long. Geoffrey of Monmouth, the chronicler whose *Historia regum Britanniae (History of the Kings of Britain)*, written before 1147, founded the legend of Arthur as we know it. Geoffrey of Monmouth wrote that Arthur had his headquarters at Caerlon in Wales. He does not mention the name Camelot at all: the first person to do so was the French poet Chrétien de Troyes, writing some two decades later.

Romantic traditions

Sir Thomas Malory, whose *Morte d'Arthur*, completed in 1470, summed up all the romantic traditions that had grown up around the king, placed Camelot at Winchester, which had been the English

Ideal location
Cadbury Hill in Somerset, England, has long been considered the most likely geographical location for King Arthur's legendary Camelot.

capital under the Wessex dynasty that included King Alfred. The city of Winchester also possessed a relic that was claimed to be the original Round Table, which may still be seen today.

In all probability Chrétien de Troyes simply invented the name Camelot. But it is a surprise, or an extraordinary coincidence, that the best candidate for the historical Arthur's seat should be near the River Cam and villages named Queen Camel and West Camel in Somerset in the southwest of England.

Regal hill

This site is Cadbury Hill, a 250-feet-high natural hill landscaped by its Iron Age occupants into a formidable defensive position, topped by 18 acres of almost flat ground that would support a sizable settlement — as indeed it did for about 3,000 years, from the Stone Age until it was razed by the Romans in around A.D. 70. It was reoccupied and strengthened some time between A.D. 460 and A.D.

The legend continues
A detail from "Arthur in Avalon," by Sir Edward Burne-Jones (1833–96), showing King Arthur's death.

500 — the very period when the historical Arthur was active. A garrison of some 1,000 people lived there, and even though there was no turreted castle with colorful pennants fluttering from the battlements, there was a huge timber hall. The spot where this settlement once stood is known locally as Arthur's Palace.

Other legends support the theory that the prototype of the mythical Arthur was based in this place. One legend tells that Arthur and his knights lie sleeping in a cavern beneath the hill, and that on one night each year the gates open, and they can be seen. Cadbury looks out over the Vale of Avalon to Glastonbury Tor, beside which the grave of Arthur was supposedly discovered in 1191.

City of dreams

There is no certainty that Cadbury is the site of the "real" Camelot. Perhaps there is no need for such certainty. The legend of Arthur, which Malory called "the matter of Britain," and its golden, dream-city of Camelot, are more powerful as myth than any heap of ancient stones or windswept hillside could ever be.

Atmospheric cave
Many locations have been suggested as possible sites for the exploits of King Arthur, his knights, and his mystical adviser, Merlin. This photograph shows the inside of "Merlin's Cave" in Tintagel, Cornwall, southwest England.

> "For there is nothing in it as it seems Saving the King; tho' some there be that hold The King a shadow, and the city real…. They are building still, seeing the city is built To music, therefore never built at all, Therefore built for ever."

Alfred, Lord Tennyson (1809–92), describing Camelot

137

THE SECRET CITIES OF TIBET

Legends of secret cities of gold with opulent palaces and wonderful inventions, inhabited by sages with mystic powers, have served over the centuries to pull explorers to the East.

WESTERNERS HAVE ALWAYS been fascinated with the "mysterious East." Travelers brave enough to risk the dangers of the Silk Road, which linked the two great civilizations of Rome and China, told tales of the unbelievable wonders they had seen there.

Tibet, situated inaccessibly high in the mountain ranges of the Himalayas, has always seemed the most likely candidate for an exotic land of wonders. In 1278 Marco Polo visited the country. In the 17th century, a Jesuit missionary to Tibet and China, Stephen Cacella, told of the existence of a mysterious land called Xembala (now known as Shambhala). Many Western explorers have long sought this legendary place in Tibet. In the 20th century, it has become synonymous with Shangri-La — a utopian Tibetan community of eternal youth and peace invented by the English writer James Hilton in his novel *Lost Horizon* (1933).

Remote monasteries

As the British Empire in India expanded during the 18th century, British explorers visited Tibet by crossing the Himalayan passes from India. Among them were Bogle and Hamilton in 1774 and Thomas Manning in 1810.

During the latter part of the 19th and the early 20th century, Western explorers made extended expeditions into Nepal and Tibet, and found places there that fitted more or less with the legendary descriptions of the secret cities. In the Tibetan capital, Lhasa, was the great monastery called the Potala, the seat of the dalai lama. Here, and at other more remote monasteries, Western visitors made contact with Tibetan lamas (priests) who astounded the Western visitors with their amazing feats of power and endurance. These feats were reportedly made possible by techniques of control of the human body taught by a Tibetan version of Tantric Buddhism.

Amazing tales

When Westerners returned home, they brought with them modern versions of the old tales of wonder. These they recounted in books that were snapped up by an avid public. For example, in her *Magic and Mystery in Tibet* (1929), the French explorer and mystic scholar Alexandra David-Neel recounted feats she had seen performed by Tibetan monks. Among these monks

were the *lung-gom-pas*, athletes who
could perform great feats of speed and
distance running. David-Neel claimed
that they could run, in a trance, non-stop
for a period of 48 hours, covering 200
miles in a day. To perform these feats,
the monks had learned to use *chi*, the
mysterious energy that is still used in
the Far East today by practitioners of
traditional oriental medicine, magic,
geomancy, and the martial arts.

The Vril-ya, fiction or fact?

More speculation about the "lost cities"
came from literary fiction. In his early
science-fiction novel, *The Coming Race*
(1871), Lord Bulwer-Lytton wrote of
secret underground cities inhabited by

> **Lord Bulwer-Lytton
> wrote of secret under-
> ground cities inhabited by
> a race of superhumans,
> the Vril-ya.**

a race of superhumans, the Vril-ya. These
people were "originally not only of our
human race, but...descended from the
same ancestors as the great Aryan family
from which...has flowed the dominant
civilization of the world." Their level of
civilization, it appears, was quite different
from that of the 19th century, for the Vril-
ya had mastered the use of a mysterious
power called *vril*. As Lord Bulwer-Lytton
described it, this power was very similar
to the chi used in the Far East.

Benevolent dictatorship

Lord Bulwer-Lytton's account, although
fictional, suggested a civilization deeply
influenced by the nature of vril. It was
such a powerful force that it had made
conflict obsolete because of the certainty
of mutual annihilation. This same energy
had also removed the point of personal
ambition, and with it the need for any
democratic system of government, which
was replaced by benevolent dictatorship
for life. This was one of several aspects
of the society that made it attractive as a
model to the Nazi movement that rose
to power in 1930's Germany.

THE NAZIS AND THE LOST CITIES

Secret cities populated with peoples who would usher in a New Order on earth — this occult belief found favor with some members of the Nazi party.

A CURIOUS PROPHECY by a being calling himself the King of the World was alleged to have appeared mysteriously in 1890 in a temple at Narabanchinii Huryee, Outer Mongolia. It predicted earthquakes, famine, war, and destruction over the following 50 years (1890–1940), culminating in a catastrophe after which the peoples of the "lost city" of Agharthi would come up from the underworld to the earth's surface. This people would re-establish the Atlantean civilization, ushering in a New Order on earth.

This prophecy was taken seriously by some members of the German Nazi movement who had developed an interest in the occult. They saw themselves as the bringers of this New Order.

Current thinking
Before the First World War, a "Vril Society" had been formed in Germany. Its members believed Lord Bulwer-Lytton's fictional novel, *The Coming Race* (1871), to contain substantial elements of truth. They followed the Theosophist C. W. Leadbeater who wrote of vril under another name: "etheric current." This, he claimed, could be directed for good or ill, bringing potentially limitless power to its users. The Vril Society was formed to investigate this power.

Karl Haushofer was a leading member of the Vril Society, and a significant figure in Nazi occultism who became an associate and adviser of Adolf Hitler. Haushofer had traveled in Tibet with the Swedish explorer Sven Hedin. He adapted Theosophical theories in his claims that the ancient civilization of the Himalayas was the forerunner of what he called the "Indo-Germanic Race," and that it would soon arise again to fulfill its destiny of world domination.

When the Nazis took power in Germany in 1933, they began to sponsor anything that would further their ideological aims. In that year, the *Deutsche Ahnenerbe* (German Ancestral Heritage Organization) came into being to study a wide range of esoteric subjects. In 1935, Heinrich Himmler made the Ahnenerbe an official organization headed by the prehistorian Wilhelm Teudt. In 1939, it was incorporated into the S.S.

Expeditions to Tibet
Some authorities who claim to be experts on the shadowy subject of Nazi occultism have suggested that, between 1939 and 1943, when the tide of the Second World War turned against Germany, there were a number of Nazi expeditions to Tibet. The alleged objective was to try to make direct contact with the World Wise Masters. The course of history suggests that the Nazi occultists were unsuccessful in this bid, and had entirely misjudged their role as the heralds of the New Order.

The Nazis ignored, however, unappealing features of the civilization. As described in the book, the society was dominated by females, who displayed a "boastful superiority in physical strength and intellectual abilities." The narrator made it absolutely clear that he could not advise the commonwealths of the Vril-ya "as an ideal form of political society."

Shortly after *The Coming Race* was published in 1871, the Russian occultist Madame Helena Petrovna Blavatsky founded a new spiritual system called Theosophy, which, she claimed, would lead to the dawn of a new age. Madame Blavatsky claimed to have made contact in the Himalayas with superbeings bearing a suspicious resemblance to Lord Bulwer-Lytton's Vril-ya. She believed that these Masters lived in "lost cities," and guarded the secret knowledge of their ancestors, the Atlanteans.

Place of healing
It is possible that the origin of such "lost city" tales was nothing more than a garbled version of stories about the Monastery of the Iron Mountain, Changpori, at Lhasa. Founded in the 17th century by the fifth dalai lama's regent, Desi Sangye Gyatso, Changpori was known as the spiritual center for Tibetan medicine. Throughout Tibet and surrounding Buddhist lands, it was a place of pilgrimage for healers, who appeared to have learned their remarkable techniques there.

Before Changpori was totally destroyed by Chinese troops in 1959, the medical teachings of the Monastery of the Iron Mountain were

Hidden kingdom
A mandala, a sacred circular Tibetan painting, showing the king of Shambhala at the center of his kingdom. This supposedly lies hidden in the mountainous north of Tibet.

famed throughout central Asia. Certain renowned medical lamas were held in the greatest esteem, bearing titles usually reserved for *bodhisattvas* (Buddhist saints): King of the World, King of the Gods, and All-Knowing One. It is possible that the fame of these teachers and their grandiose titles were misunderstood by people in the West, leading to the myth of the super-beings that is a central belief of Theosophy.

Theosophical thought indicated that the lost city of Shambhala was located on part of an earth energy grid of "etheric current" that runs across the continents of Asia and Europe from east to west. They believed that this energy connects in some mystic way with the holy mountains of the Aryans. These are Mount El'brus in the Caucasus, Mount Belukha in the Altai Range on the C.I.S.–Mongolia border, and Mount Pamir in the Pamir Range, Tadzhikistan.

The Theosophists claimed that the Aryans' civilization was situated in what is now the Gobi Desert. It was wiped out in a disaster of massive proportions. The few survivors, so the story goes, fled west to the Caucasus and from there to Scandinavia. Those who did not travel westward descended into caves beneath the Himalayas. These were the World Wise Masters. They divided into two factions, one following the right-hand path of magic and the other the left-hand. The first was centered at Shambhala, and the other at Agharthi.

Catastrophic outcome

Madame Blavatsky claimed that her Oriental mentor, Mahatma Koot Hoomi, had informed her that following a series of natural catastrophes and wars, the guardians of Shambhala, led by the "King of the World," will emerge from the underworld. Then they will organize the elite to set up a "New Order" on the planet. This tale became a theme in Nazi occult thought — the Nazis becoming the elite in the New Order. The Nazis sought the world domination of the path of Agharthi, not the path of enlightenment that was the goal of Shambhala.

Journeys to Tibet

In 1904, an invasion by the British Army under Sir Francis Younghusband opened up Tibet to the Western world. This event gave more adventurous Theosophists a chance to seek the abode of the World Wise Masters. Among these explorers was the Russian painter and mystic Nikolay Roerich. In the book he wrote concerning his experiences there, *The Himalayas? Abode of Light* (1947), Roerich stated that the foothills of the Himalayas conceal entrances to the underworld. Vast underground galleries, he claimed, lead deep beneath Kanchenjunga, whose name (meaning "The Five Sacred Treasures of the Great Snow") is said to refer to the treasures of the lost underground city of Agharthi.

Unfortunately, despite further investigations, no secret underground cities have yet been found. If they do exist outside the fantastic realms of the imagination, the treasures (or terrors) of Shambhala and Agharthi remain hidden beneath the snows of the Himalayas.

> ## Nikolay Roerich stated that the foothills of the Himalayas conceal entrances to the underworld.

Mystical palace
Potala Palace, the seat of the dalai lama, overlooking the Tibetan capital, Lhasa.

Symbolic image
Russian explorer Nikolay Roerich in Ulaan Baatar, Mongolia, in 1927. The symbol on the banner he is holding represents the secret world of Shambhala.

INDEX

Page numbers in **bold** type refer to illustrations and captions.

PHOTOGRAPHIC SOURCES

Aerofilms Ltd.: 8-9; **Ancient Art and Architecture Collection**: 73, 107tr, 111b, 117t; **Archiv für Kunst und Geschichte**: 7c, 65t, 81b, 86-7 background, 86l, 87br; **Australian Overseas Information Service**, London: 33b; **John Beckett**: 116tl, r; **Bodleian Library**: 117b; **Bridgeman Art Library**: 1, 6tl, 35l, 63b, 64l, 74b, 82, 90t, 110t, 114r, 125b, 130b, 131tr, 134b, 136t, 137t; Reproduced by courtesy of the Trustees of the **British Library**: 115t, 130t; Reproduced by courtesy of the Trustees of the **British Museum**: 14, 15t, b, 16t, bl, br, 17, 18, 21r, 38l, 57, 60tl, 61, 62, 63t, 64r, 114b, 125t; Cast supplied by **British Museum Connections**: cover; **Jean-Loup Charmet**: 34, 84t, 85t, 132t; **Peter Clayton Associates**: 68l, r, 69c; **Bruce Coleman Ltd.**: 31r (N. Devore), 39l (Mackinnon), 92t (J. Simon), 102 (C. Zuber); **Paul Devereux**: 93tr; **C.M. Dixon**: 6b, 65b, 72t, 74t, 75, 84b, 106bl, 108-9; **Jeremy Dixon and Edward Jones**: 54l; **The Egyptian Museum**, Cairo: 70l; **E.T. Archive**: 26, 94-5t, 99t; **Mary Evans Picture Library**: 27t, 35tr, 40l, 41l, 42l, 48l, 122t, 126l; **Werner Forman Archive**: 27b, 28b, 60bl, 91b, 92l, 93l, 135t (R.Aberman), b; **Fortean Picture Library**: 91t, 136b, 137b (P. Broadhurst); **Photographie Giraudon**: 24t; **Sonia Halliday**: 71r, 72b, 134t (J. Simson); **Robert Harding Picture Library**: 28t, 29b, 47b (J.G. Ross), 48r, 83b, 94bl, 95br, 103b (J.G. Ross), 124b, 141t (N. Blythe); **Michael Holford**: 37r, 38r, 78t, 79b, 80t, 85b, 90b, 131b; **Hulton Deutsch Collection**: 19b, 129t; **Image Bank**: 44-5 (A. Choisnet), 44t (D. Jeffrey), 45t (H. Wendler), 46b (J. Rajs), 47t (D. Hamilton), 96t (N.Pavloff), 99b (T.O. Edmunds); **Images Colour Library**: 43r, 54tr, 55tl, 56, 86tr, 100; Based on original illustrations by the author, Peter Hodges, from *How the Pyramids Were Built*, 1989, Element Books, Longmead,

Shaftesbury, Dorset © **Julian Keeble** 1989: 50-53; **Kinema Collection**: 66c; **Kobal Collection**: 66t, b, 67; **Mansell Collection**: 25t, 86br, 118tl; **National Maritime Museum**, Greenwich: 115b; **Peter Newark's Pictures**: 39r, 40r, 41r; **Nigel Pennick**: 87tr; **Popperfoto**: 32l; **Réunion des Musées Nationaux/Musée Guimet**: 140; **Nicholas Roerich Museum**: 141b; **Scala**: 123t; Trustees of the **Science Museum**: 110b, 111t; Reproduced by permission of **Prof. N.J.D. Smith**, King's College School of Medicine and Dentistry: 69r; **South American Pictures**/Tony Morrison: 2 (inset), 132b, 133; **Frank Spooner Pictures/Gamma**: 42r (Contrast), 43l (Liaison/Schwartz), 54br (Vidward), 55tr (A. Seitz), 55bl & br (Liaison/S. Kagan), 58-9 (Gaillarde-Francolon), 60r (Figaro/Laubier), 92-3 background (Boisberranger/Bezia), 96l, 101r (C. Angel), 103t (J.M. Adamini), 116r (Gaillarde-Francolon); **Syndication International**: 123b, 124t; **The Telegraph, Alton, Ill.**: 35br; **Topkapi Saray Museum**, Istanbul: 112l; **David Towersey**: 122b; **Jim Winker/Rekwin Co.**: 118r; **Zefa**: 24b (Puttkamer), 25b (Bachmann), 29t, 32r (R. Smith), 33t (Teasy), 92br, 97b (Y. Limen), 98t (Damm), b, 129c (F. Lanting), 138-9 background (Hackenberg).

b - bottom; c - center; t - top;
r - right; l - left.

Efforts have been made to contact the holder of the copyright for each picture. In several cases these have been untraceable, for which we offer our apologies.